THE HISTORY PLAYS AND POEMS OF
WILLIAM SHAKESPEARE

THE HISTORY PLAYS AND POEMS OF

WILLIAM SHAKESPEARE

EDITED BY KATHLEEN KUIPER, SENIOR EDITOR, ARTS AND CULTURE

Britannica
Educational Publishing

IN ASSOCIATION WITH

ROSEN
EDUCATIONAL SERVICES

Published in 2013 by Britannica Educational Publishing
(a trademark of Encyclopædia Britannica, Inc.)
in association with Rosen Educational Services, LLC
29 East 21st Street, New York, NY 10010.

Distributed exclusively by Rosen Educational Services.
For a listing of additional Britannica Educational Publishing titles, call toll free (800) 237-9932.

First Edition

Britannica Educational Publishing
Adam Augustyn: Assistant Manager
J.E. Luebering: Senior Manager
Marilyn L. Barton: Senior Coordinator, Production Control
Steven Bosco: Director, Editorial Technologies
Lisa S. Braucher: Senior Producer and Data Editor
Yvette Charboneau: Senior Copy Editor
Kathy Nakamura: Manager, Media Acquisition
Kathleen Kuiper: Senior Editor, Arts and Culture

Rosen Educational Services
Jeanne Nagle: Senior Editor
Nelson Sá: Art Director
Cindy Reiman: Photography Manager
Amy Feinberg: Photo Researcher
Brian Garvey: Designer and Cover Design
Introduction by Adam Augustyn

Library of Congress Cataloging-in-Publication Data

The history plays and poems of William Shakespeare/edited by Kathleen Kuiper.
    p. cm. — (Shakespeare: his work and world)
Includes bibliographical references and index.
ISBN 978-1-61530-929-0 (library binding)
1. Shakespeare, William, 1564–1616 — Histories. 2. Shakespeare, William, 1564–1616 —
Poetic works. 3. Historical drama, English — History and criticism. I. Kuiper, Kathleen.
PR2982.H49 2013
822.3'3 — dc23

                                                                        2012032633

Manufactured in the United States of America

On the cover: French actor Denis Podalydes performs as the title character of William
Shakespeare's *The Life and Death of Richard the Third*, staged in 2010 as part of a theatre
festival in Avignon, France. *AFP/Getty Images*

Pages 1, 10, 35, 59, 74, 88 Hulton Archive/Getty Images

Contents

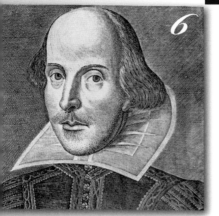

Introduction

*T*he very concept of a history play was a novel one in Shakespeare's time. For centuries, dating back to the ancient Greeks and Romans, dramas had been broadly defined as either tragedies, meaning stories of great people who are struck down by calamitous events, or comedies, which concern everyday citizens reveling in the follies of public life and end happily. History (or chronicle) plays began to be considered a discrete type of drama only in Shakespeare's England. The first example of the genre, *The Famous Victories of Henry the Fifth*, was written anonymously sometime between 1583 and 1590. History plays could be either comic, tragic, or—most commonly—a combination of both, but the genre's sole defining feature is the presentation of historic events in a chronological fashion.

As evidenced throughout this book, Shakespeare is, in many ways, the originator of the history play. He worked in the nascent genre to create works of such striking originality and depth that they came to define history plays throughout the subsequent centuries. His history oeuvre consists of two tetralogies, each of which follows a series of sequential English monarchs, as well as scattered stand-alone works that treat a historical personage over the course of a single play.

While Shakespeare's historic plays do loosely follow historical events, he takes much dramatic license with the facts in order to present more compelling stories. The

An actor returns to the stage during a 2008 production of Richard III *in Stratford-upon-Avon, Shakespeare's hometown. Cate Gillon/ Getty Images*

events of these plays are primarily accurate, but the works' focus and tone epitomize the aphorism that "history is written by the winners." An aspect of his lax treatment of the historical record is seen in the political undercurrent that creeps into some of his plays, such as the contrasting depictions of similar murders by Richard III and Henry VII. Richard is portrayed as evil and conniving while Henry—who, not coincidentally, was the founder of the Tudor dynasty and grandfather of Shakespeare's queen, Elizabeth I—is portrayed sympathetically, in deference to the powers ruling England at the time.

Shakespeare's earliest history play, *Henry VI, Part 1*, inaugurates his first tetralogy with the early years of the 15th-century reign of Henry VI. The play begins with the funeral of the title character's father, Henry V, and the newly crowned young king is soon thrust into war with France. The action of the drama alternates between court intrigue in England and the war in France. The play concludes with the Earl of Suffolk convincing Henry to marry Margaret of Anjou, which is an effort to end the war and increase the earl's influence with the king.

In *Henry VI, Part 2*, Suffolk, who has been elevated to a duke by a grateful Henry, sees his influence over Margaret (and therefore the king) deepen as the two begin an affair. The court machinations depicted in *Part 1* grow even more intense with Margaret's arrival, as the guileless Henry is unable to prevent Richard Plantagenet, the duke of York, from amassing power in the hopes of attaining the throne. Plantagenet encourages an insurrection led by Jack Cade, which is eventually put down but not before it exposes Henry's weakness. The English nobles then choose sides, and the play ends with the country on the brink of civil war.

The rivalry between the Lancasters (Henry's house) and the Yorks blossoms into the Wars of the Roses (1455–85) in *Henry VI, Part 3*. A mad and defeated Henry is unable to prevent the Yorks from seizing power, and he agrees to disinherit his son and pass the crown to the Yorks when he dies. This compromise infuriates Margaret, who subsequently defeats and kills Richard Plantagenet in battle. However, the crown remains with the Yorks as Plantagenet's son claims the throne from an ineffectual Henry and reigns as Edward IV. The two houses battle back and forth for the rest of the play, with Henry briefly regaining the throne, but the drama ends with Edward as king, Henry dead, Margaret banished, and Edward's younger brother Richard revealed as a power-hungry schemer.

Richard moves into the forefront of the action in the final play of the first tetralogy, *Richard III*. Befitting someone who fought against the forebears of one of Shakespeare's contemporary monarchs, Richard is presented as one of the greatest villains in Shakespearean drama. Although his actions throughout the play are deplorable, the character of Richard is so complex and well drawn that he is one of the most popular Shakespearean roles. (Curiously, in contrast to his image as a nefarious murderer made common by this play, the real Richard III is regarded by modern scholars as an adequate leader whose reputation was marred by propaganda.)

The play begins with a soliloquy by the deformed Richard, who expresses jealousy of his brother Edward and reveals his plan to take the throne for himself. Richard woos and marries Lady Anne, who is at first resistant to his advances since Richard had earlier killed both her husband and her father-in-law. Soon after his brother's death, Richard proceeds to kill every person who stands in his way, including the king's heirs, Richard's own two young nephews. Aided by the Duke of Buckingham, who arranges executions and spreads damning rumours about Edward and the legitimacy of his children, Richard ascends to the throne. Henry Tudor, earl of Richmond, challenges Richard's claim to the throne and gathers an army. The night before the climactic Battle of Bosworth Field, Richard is haunted by the ghosts of his victims. The next day Richmond kills Richard in combat and ascends to the throne as Henry VII.

Following his first tetralogy in the historic panoply, Shakespeare next wrote *King John*, a self-contained dramatization of the life of the title figure, the earliest monarch on whom Shakespeare centred a play. The work begins with John having recently assumed the crown against the wishes of the king of France, who demands that John's nephew Arthur become the English king. The dispute escalates into war, with John's most fearsome combatant turning out to be his brother's illegitimate son, known in the play as the Bastard. John's forces capture Arthur, who later dies in an escape attempt and becomes a rallying point for John's enemies. The war grinds to a stalemate that sees only the Bastard continuing to fight—that is, until he learns of John being poisoned by a treasonous monk. John's son Henry ascends to the throne and makes peace with the French in the play's final act.

Shakespeare's second tetralogy is notable for two reasons. The first is that it features one of the Bard's most beloved creations, the ribald soldier Sir John Falstaff. The other is that it appears out of chronological sequence with the first tetralogy, so that his re-telling of medieval English history could end with a heroic figure in Henry V, rather than his predecessor Richard III.

The first play of this series is *Richard II*, which begins with the king exiling some noblemen and seizing property from others. His actions sew discord among England's aristocracy; one of the exiled noblemen, Henry Bolingbroke, gathers an army and invades England while Richard is off fighting in Ireland. Once other nobles flock to Bolingbroke's cause, Richard is forced to surrender, and Bolingbroke is crowned Henry IV. While in prison, Richard realizes the folly of his past behaviour and gains a newfound moral strength, shortly before he is murdered.

The first years of Bolingbroke's rule are the time period covered in *Henry IV, Part 1*, but the true focus of the play is Henry's wastrel son, Prince Hal. While Henry is locked in battle with rebels throughout his kingdom, his son and his friends—including the rotund and rowdy Falstaff—drink and caper at Mistress Quickly's inn in Eastcheap. The group is on the verge of committing highway robbery as a lark when Hal is summoned to his father's side in battle. Hal makes amends with Henry on the battlefield as the son saves his father's life and kills the rebel Hotspur (whose valour Henry had previously praised in contrast to his son's former comportment). Henry's forces proceed to put down the rebellion, but only temporarily.

The rebellion is back in full force at the beginning of *Henry IV, Part 2*, with Henry's son John leading the king's forces. While John leads the battle, Hal returns to Eastcheap in disguise to spy on his old friends since he has heard that Falstaff's behaviour has grown even more decadent. A disappointed Henry then fears that his son has returned to his previous ways, but the two are reconciled once more, shortly before Henry's death. His parting advice to Hal is that the young king should seek foreign quarrels as a means of distracting the populace, thus avoiding the internal strife that plagued Henry's reign. At play's end the newly crowned Henry V shows his newfound maturity by denouncing Falstaff.

Henry V opens with the king heeding his father's dying words and declaring war on France. The majority of the play follows Henry's campaign in France; the title character is fleshed out as he attempts to live up to his new leadership role. His humanity is emphasized when, the night before the Battle of Agincourt, he disguises himself to walk among his men to better know them. Henry's heroic nature shines through during his inspirational St. Crispin's Day speech shortly before the battle. The English side emerges victorious, and Henry ends the action happily betrothed to Princess Katherine of France. However, the key final words of *Henry V* belong to the chorus, which reminds the audience that England's happiness will be short-lived, as Henry's son will oversee a country burdened by civil war.

Shakespeare's final history play was another standalone work, *Henry VIII*. The play begins with the Duke of Buckingham being convicted of treason despite doubts on the part of Henry and his wife, Katharine, that Buckingham is guilty. En route to his execution, Buckingham prophetically warns Henry to beware of false friends such as those who betrayed him.

The main thrust of the plot depicts Henry falling for Anne Bullen (Boleyn) and attempting to end his marriage to Katharine on the grounds that she had not produced a male heir to the throne. Henry separates from Katharine, but his conniving lord chancellor, Cardinal Wolsey, attempts to augment his power over the king by stopping the marriage to Anne. After Henry secretly marries Anne, Wolsey's successor furthers a plot to gain influence over Henry by accusing his trusted archbishop, Thomas Cranmer, of heresy. The play ends on a positive note as Henry finally proves resistant to manipulation and reaffirms his support of Cranmer, who then baptizes Henry's newborn daughter and prophesizes a glorious future for England during the reign of Elizabeth I.

Like his comedies and dramas, Shakespeare's history plays are noteworthy not just for their profound insights, but for the exquisite language used to convey those ideas.

Unsurprisingly, his poetic accomplishments were not limited to his blank verse alone, but to traditional poems themselves. Only two were published during his lifetime, the narrative poems *Venus and Adonis* and *The Rape of Lucrece*. His lasting poetic reputation, however, rests primarily with his unpublished sonnet sequence.

Shakespeare's sonnets are often regarded as the highest quality work produced in that particular poetic form. In fact, Shakespeare himself has sometimes been referred to as not only the greatest dramatist of all time but the greatest poet ever as well, owing to the quality of his sonnets. His name has become synonymous with the English sonnet form, which has a characteristic rhyming scheme of *abab cdcd efef gg*. His sonnets are addressed to either a "fair youth" (a male friend, possibly the earl of Southampton, with whom Shakespeare shared an intense platonic connection) or a "dark lady" (a potentially fictional lover). The works not only touch on the standard sonnet subject of love, but also broader themes such as time, fame, and death. Shakespeare used his poetry—as he did his drama—not only to entertain and enrapture his audience, but to plumb the depths of human existence to a degree that few, if any, other artists ever have.

Chapter 1

THE DATING AND PUBLICATION OF SHAKESPEARE'S PLAYS

*D*espite much scholarly argument, it is often impossible to date a given play by William Shakespeare precisely. But there is a general consensus, especially for plays written in the spans 1588–1601 and 1605–07, and from 1609 onward. Dates of composition have been based on external and internal evidence, general stylistic and thematic considerations, and the observation that an output of no more than two plays a year seems to have been established in those periods when dating is clearer than others.

Shakespeare's two narrative poems, *Venus and Adonis* and *The Rape of Lucrece*, can be dated with certainty to the years when the plague stopped dramatic performances in London—in 1592–93 and 1593–94, respectively—just before their publication. But the sonnets offer many and various problems; they cannot have been written all at one time. Most scholars set them within the period 1593–1600. "The Phoenix and the Turtle" ("Turtle" here meaning turtledove) can be dated 1600–01.

PUBLICATION IN THE ELIZABETHAN ERA

Acting companies in London during the Renaissance were perennially in search of new plays. They usually paid on a piecework basis, to freelance writers. Shakespeare was an important exception. As a member of Lord Chamberlain's

Men and then the King's Men, he wrote for his company as a sharer in their capitalist enterprise.

The companies were not eager to sell their plays to publishers, especially when the plays were still popular and in the repertory. At certain times, however, the companies might be impelled to do so, as when a company disbanded or when it was put into enforced inactivity by visitations of the plague, or when the plays were no longer current. (The companies owned the plays; the individual authors had no intellectual property rights once the plays had been sold to the actors.)

Such plays were usually published in quarto form—that is, printed on both sides of large sheets of paper with four printed pages on each side. When the sheet was folded twice and bound, it yielded eight printed pages to each "gathering." A few plays were printed in octavo, with the sheet being folded thrice and yielding 16 smaller printed pages to each gathering.

SHAKESPEARE'S PUBLISHED PLAYS

Half of Shakespeare's plays were printed in quarto (at least one in octavo) during his lifetime. Occasionally a play was issued in a seemingly unauthorized volume—that is, not having been regularly sold by the company to the publisher. The acting company might then commission its own authorized version. The quarto title page of *Romeo and Juliet* (1599), known today as the second quarto, declares that it is "Newly corrected, augmented, and amended, as it hath been sundry times publicly acted by the Right Honorable the Lord Chamberlain His Servants." The second quarto of *Hamlet* (1604–05) similarly advertises itself as "Newly imprinted and enlarged to almost as much again as it was, according to the true and perfect copy." Indeed, the first quarto of *Hamlet* (1603) is considerably shorter

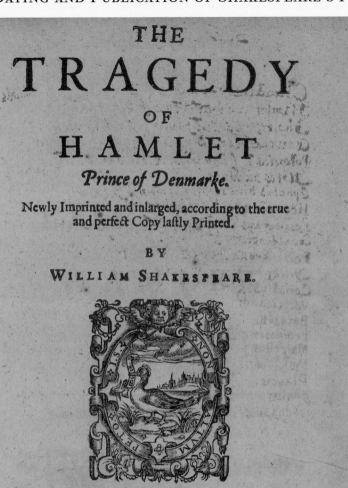

THE

TRAGEDY

OF

HAMLET

Prince of Denmarke.

Newly Imprinted and inlarged, according to the true
and perfect Copy lastly Printed.

BY

WILLIAM SHAKESPEARE.

LONDON,

Printed by *W. S.* for *Iohn Smethwicke*, and are to be sold at his
Shop in Saint *Dunstans* Church-yard in Fleetstreet:
Vnder the Diall.

Title page to an early edition of Shakespeare's Hamlet. *The New York Public Library/Art Resource, NY*

than the second, and the first quarto of *Romeo and Juliet* lacks some 800 lines found in its successor. Both contain what appear to be misprints or other errors that are then corrected in the second quarto. The first quarto of *Love's Labour's Lost* (1598) presents itself as "Newly corrected and

PLAYS INTO PRINT

The Stationers' Company was formed in 1403 from the old fraternities of scriveners (professional copyists), limners (manuscript illuminators), bookbinders, and stationers (booksellers). In 1557 it was granted a charter that gave it a virtual monopoly. Thereafter, only those who were members of the company or who otherwise had special privileges or patents might print matter for sale in the kingdom.

Controls were tightened in 1586, when printing was confined to London, except for one press each in the universities of Oxford and Cambridge. Some landmark publications of the period were John Lyly's *Euphues*, published by Gabriel Cawood (1578); Sir Thomas North's translation of Plutarch's *Lives*, so important for Shakespeare, by Thomas Vautroullier (1579); Edmund Spenser's *Faerie Queene*, by William Ponsonbie (1589–96), and the Authorised (or King James) Version of the Bible (1611).

Publication of drama was left, along with much of the poetry and the popular literature, to publishers who were not members of the Stationers' Company and to the outright pirates, who scrambled for what they could get and but for whom much would never have been printed. To join this fringe, the would-be publisher had only to get hold of a manuscript, by fair means or foul, enter it as his copy (or dispense with the formality), and have it printed. Just such a man was Thomas Thorpe, the publisher of Shakespeare's sonnets (1609). The mysterious "Mr. W.H." in the dedication is thought by some to be the person who procured him his copy. The first Shakespeare play to be published (*Titus Andronicus*, 1594) was printed by a notorious pirate, John Danter, who also brought out, anonymously, a defective *Romeo and Juliet* (1597), largely from shorthand notes made during performance. Eighteen of the plays appeared in "good" and "bad" quartos before the great First Folio in 1623. A typical imprint of the time, of the "good" second quarto of *Hamlet* (1604), reads: "Printed by I.R. for N.L. and are to be sold at his shoppe under Saint Dunston's Church in Fleetstreet"; i.e., printed by James Roberts for Nicholas Ling. For the First Folio, a large undertaking of more than 900 pages, a syndicate of five was formed, headed by Edward Blount and William Jaggard. The Folio was printed, none too well, by Jaggard's son, Isaac.

augmented," implying perhaps that it, too, corrects an earlier, unauthorized version of the play, though none today is known to exist.

GENESIS OF UNAUTHORIZED EDITIONS

The status of the seemingly unauthorized editions is much debated today. The older view of A. W. Pollard, W. W. Greg, Fredson Bowers, and other practitioners of the so-called New Bibliography generally regards these texts as suspect and perhaps pirated, either by unscrupulous visitors to the theatre or by minor actors who took part in performance and who then were paid to reconstruct the plays from memory. The unauthorized texts do contain elements that sound like the work of eyewitnesses or actors (and are valuable for that reason). In some instances, the unauthorized text is notably closer to the authorized text when certain minor actors are onstage than at other times, suggesting that these actors may have been involved in a memorial reconstruction. Both *Henry VI, Part 2* and *Henry VI, Part 3* originally appeared in shorter versions that may have been memorially reconstructed by actors.

MR. WILLIAM
SHAKESPEARES

COMEDIES,
HISTORIES, &
TRAGEDIES.

Publiſhed according to the True Originall Copies.

Frontispiece to the First Folio, the first collection of Shakespeare's works to be published together. The selection was made after his death by his theatre colleagues. Rischgitz/Hulton Archive/Getty Images

A revisionary school of textual criticism that gained favour in the latter part of the 20th century argued that these texts might have been earlier versions with their own theatrical rationale and that they should be regarded as part of a theatrical process by which the plays evolved onstage. Certainly the situation varies from quarto to quarto, and unquestionably the unauthorized quartos are valuable to the understanding of stage history.

Several years after Shakespeare died in 1616, colleagues of his in the King's Men, John Heminge and Henry Condell, undertook the assembling of a collected edition. It appeared in 1623 as *Mr. William Shakespeare's Comedies, Histories, and Tragedies, Published According to the True Original Copies*. It did not contain the poems and left out *Pericles* as perhaps of uncertain authorship. Nor did it include *The Two Noble Kinsmen, Edward III*, the portion of *The Book of Sir Thomas More* that Shakespeare may have contributed, or the *Cardenio* that Shakespeare appears to have written with John Fletcher and that may have provided the basis for Lewis Theobald's *Double Falsehood* in 1727. It did nonetheless include 36 plays, half of them appearing in print for the first time.

COLLECTING SHAKESPEARE'S WORKS

Heminge and Condell had the burdensome task of choosing what materials to present to the printer, for they had on hand a number of authorial manuscripts, other documents that had served as promptbooks for performance (these were especially valuable since they bore the license for performance), and some 18 plays that had appeared in print. Fourteen of these had been published in what the editors regarded as more or less reliable texts (though only two were used unaltered): *Titus Andronicus*; *Romeo and Juliet* (the second quarto); *Richard II*; *Richard*

Bust of Shakespeare in London, underneath which is a stone replica of the First Folio, published by John Heminge and Henry Condell.
© Loop Images/SuperStock

III; *Love's Labour's Lost*; *Henry IV, Part 1*; *Henry IV, Part 2*; *A Midsummer Night's Dream*; *The Merchant of Venice*; *Much Ado About Nothing*; *Hamlet*; *King Lear*; *Troilus and Cressida*; and *Othello*. *Henry VI, Part 1* and *Henry VI, Part 2* had been published in quarto in shortened form and under different titles (*The First Part of the Contention Betwixt the Two Famous*

Houses of York and Lancaster and *The True Tragedy of Richard Duke of York*) but were not used in this form by Heminge and Condell for the 1623 Folio.

Much was discovered by textual scholarship after Heminge and Condell did their original work, and the result was a considerable revision in what came to be regarded as the best choice of original text from which an editor ought to work. In plays published both in folio and quarto (or octavo) format, the task of choosing was immensely complicated. *King Lear* especially became a critical battleground in which editors argued for the superiority of various features of the 1608 quarto or the folio text. The two differ substantially and must indeed represent different stages of composition and of staging, so that both are germane to an understanding of the play's textual and theatrical history. The same is true of *Hamlet*, with its unauthorized quarto of 1603, its corrected quarto of 1604–05, and the folio text, all significantly at variance with one another. Other plays in which the textual relationship of quarto to folio is highly problematic include *Troilus and Cressida*; *Othello*; *Henry IV, Part 2*; *Henry VI, Part 1* and *Henry VI, Part 2*; *The Merry Wives of Windsor*; *Henry V*; and *A Midsummer Night's Dream*.

Most of the cases where there are both quarto and folio originals are problematic in some interesting way. Individual situations are too complex to be described here, but information is readily available in critical editions of Shakespeare's plays and poems, especially in *The Oxford Shakespeare*, in a collected edition and in individual critical editions; *The New Cambridge Shakespeare*; and the third series of *The Arden Shakespeare*.

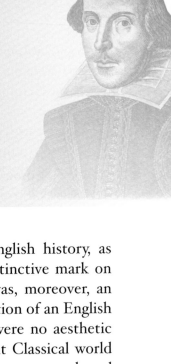

Chapter 2

THE EARLY HISTORIES

*I*n Shakespeare's explorations of English history, as in romantic comedy, he put his distinctive mark on a genre and made it his. The genre was, moreover, an unusual one. There was as yet no definition of an English history (or chronicle) play, and there were no aesthetic rules regarding its shaping. The ancient Classical world had recognized two broad categories of genre, comedy and tragedy. (This account leaves out more specialized genres like the satyr play.) Over centuries, Aristotle and other critics, including Horace, had evolved Classical definitions. Tragedy dealt with the disaster-struck lives of great people, was written in elevated verse, and took as its setting a mythological and ancient world of gods and heroes: Agamemnon, Theseus, Oedipus, Medea, and the rest. Pity and terror were the prevailing emotional responses in plays that sought to understand, however imperfectly, the will of the supreme gods. Classical comedy, conversely, dramatized the everyday. Its chief figures were citizens of Athens and Rome—householders, courtesans, slaves, scoundrels, and so forth. The humour was immediate, contemporary, topical; the lampooning was satirical, even savage. Members of the audience were invited to look at representations of their own daily lives, and to laugh at greed and folly.

The English history play had no such ideal theoretical structure. It was an existential invention; the dramatic treatment of recent English history. It might be tragic or comic or, more commonly, a hybrid. (In act two of Shakespeare's *Hamlet,* the character Polonius captures the ludicrous potential for endless hybridizations: "tragedy, comedy, history, pastoral, pastoral-comical, historical-pastoral, tragical-historical, tragical-comical-historical-pastoral..."). Shakespeare's history plays were so successful in the 1590s' London theatre that in 1623, the editors of the playwright's complete works chose to group his dramatic output under three headings: comedies, histories, and tragedies. The genre established itself by sheer force of its compelling popularity.

In 1590 or thereabouts, Shakespeare had really only one viable model for the English history play, an anonymous and sprawling drama called *The Famous Victories of Henry the Fifth* (1583–88). That play told the saga of Henry IV's son, Prince Hal, from the days of his adolescent rebellion down through his victory over the French at the Battle of Agincourt in 1415—in other words, the material that Shakespeare would later use in writing three major plays, *Henry IV, Part 1; Henry IV, Part 2;* and *Henry V.* Shakespeare chose to start not with Prince Hal but with more recent history in the reign of Henry V's son Henry VI, as well as the civil wars that saw the overthrow of Henry VI by Edward IV, and then the accession to power in 1483 of Richard III. This material proved to be so rich in themes and dramatic conflicts that he wrote four plays on it, a "tetralogy" extending from *Henry VI* in three parts (c. 1589–93) to *Richard III* (c. 1592–94).

These plays were immediately successful. Contemporary references indicate that audiences of the early 1590s thrilled to the story (in *Henry VI, Part 1*) of the brave

Lord Talbot doing battle in France against the witch Joan of Arc and her lover, the French Dauphin, but being undermined in his heroic effort by effeminacy and corruption at home. Henry VI himself is, as Shakespeare portrays him, a weak king, raised to the kingship by the early death of his father, incapable of controlling factionalism in his court, and enervated personally by his infatuation with a dangerous Frenchwoman, Margaret of Anjou. Henry VI is cuckolded by his wife and her lover, the Duke of Suffolk, and (in *Henry VI, Part 2*) proves unable to defend his virtuous uncle, the Duke of Gloucester, against opportunistic

Actors from Stratford's Royal Shakespeare Company rehearse a fight scene between Joan Purcell and Talbot from Henry VI, Part 1, *in 2008. Cate Gillon/Getty Images*

enemies. The result is civil unrest, lower-class rebellion (led by Jack Cade), and eventually all-out civil war between the Lancastrian faction, nominally headed by Henry VI, and the Yorkist claimants under the leadership of Edward IV and his brothers.

Richard III completes the saga with its account of the baleful rise of Richard of Gloucester through the murdering of his brother the Duke of Clarence and of Edward IV's two sons, who were also Richard's nephews. Richard's tyrannical reign yields eventually and inevitably to the newest and most successful claimant of the throne, Henry Tudor, earl of Richmond. This is the man who becomes Henry VII, scion of the Tudor dynasty and grandfather of Queen Elizabeth I, who reigned from 1558 to 1603 and hence during the entire first decade and more of Shakespeare's productive career.

The Shakespearean English history play told of the country's history at a time when the English nation was struggling with its own sense of national identity and experiencing a new sense of power. Queen Elizabeth had brought stability and a relative freedom from war to her decades of rule. She had held at bay the Roman Catholic powers of the Continent, notably Philip II of Spain, and, with the help of a storm at sea, had fought off Philip's attempts to invade her kingdom with the great Spanish Armada of 1588. In England the triumph of the nation was viewed universally as a divine deliverance. The second edition of Raphael Holinshed's *Chronicles* was at hand as a vast source for Shakespeare's historical playwriting. It, too, celebrated the emergence of England as a major Protestant power, led by a popular and astute monarch.

From the perspective of the 1590s, the history of the 15th century also seemed newly pertinent. England had emerged from a terrible civil war in 1485, with Henry Tudor's victory over Richard III at the Battle of Bosworth

Field. The chief personages of these wars, known as the Wars of the Roses—Henry Tudor, Richard III, the duke of Buckingham, Hastings, Rivers, Gray, and many more—were very familiar to contemporary English readers.

Because these historical plays of Shakespeare in the early 1590s were so intent on telling the saga of emergent nationhood, they exhibit a strong tendency to identify villains and heroes. Shakespeare is writing dramas, not schoolbook texts, and he freely alters dates, facts, and emphases. Lord Talbot in *Henry VI, Part 1* is a hero because he dies defending English interests against the corrupt French. In *Henry VI, Part 2* Humphrey, duke of Gloucester, is cut down by opportunists because he represents the best interests of the commoners and the nation as a whole. Most of all, Richard of Gloucester is made out to be a villain epitomizing the very worst features of a chaotic century of civil strife. He foments strife, lies, and murders and makes outrageous promises he has no intention of keeping. He is a brilliantly theatrical figure because he is so inventive and clever, but he is also deeply threatening. Shakespeare gives him every defect that popular tradition imagined: a hunchback; a baleful (evil), glittering eye; a conspiratorial genius.

The real Richard was no such villain, it seems. At least, his politically inspired murders were no worse than the systematic elimination of all opposition by his successor, the historical Henry VII. The difference is that Henry VII lived to commission historians to tell the story his way, whereas Richard lost everything through defeat. As founder of the Tudor dynasty and grandfather of Queen Elizabeth, Henry VII could command a respect that even Shakespeare was bound to honour, and accordingly the Henry Tudor that he portrays at the end of *Richard III* is a God-fearing patriot and loving husband of the Yorkist princess who is to give birth to the next generation of Tudor monarchs.

Richard III is a tremendous play, both in length and in the bravura depiction of its titular protagonist. It is called a tragedy on its original title page, as are other of these early English history plays. Certainly they present us with brutal deaths and with instructive falls of great men from positions of high authority to degradation and misery. Yet these plays are not tragedies in the Classical sense of the term. They contain so much else, and notably they end on a major key, namely the accession to power of the Tudor dynasty that will give England its great years under Elizabeth. The story line is one of suffering and of eventual salvation, of deliverance by mighty forces of history and of divine oversight that will not allow England to continue to suffer once she has returned to the true path of duty and decency. In this important sense, the early history plays are like tragicomedies or romances.

HENRY VI, PART 1

Henry VI, Part 1 is the first in a sequence of four history plays (the others being *Henry VI, Part 2*, *Henry VI, Part 3*, and *Richard III*). Shakespeare's primary sources for the historical events in this play and the others in the sequence were the chronicles of Edward Hall and Raphael Holinshed.

Part 1 begins at the funeral of Henry V, as political factions are forming around the boy king, Henry VI. The chief rivalry is between Henry's uncle Humphrey, duke of Gloucester, the Lord Protector, and his great-uncle, Henry Beaufort, bishop of Winchester. The peace Henry V had established in France is shattered as Joan la Pucelle (Joan of Arc) persuades the newly crowned French king, Charles VII, to reclaim French lands held by the English. Most of

Portrait of the real King Henry VI, the subject of Shakespeare's first history play. Archive Photos/Getty Images

THE REAL HENRY VI

(b. Dec. 6, 1421, Windsor, Berkshire, Eng. — d. May 21/22, 1471, London)

Henry succeeded his father, Henry V, on Sept. 1, 1422, and on the death (Oct. 21, 1422) of his maternal grandfather, the French king Charles VI, Henry was proclaimed king of France in accordance with the terms of the Treaty of Troyes (1420) made after Henry V's French victories.

Henry's minority was never officially ended, but from 1437 he was considered old enough to rule for himself, and his personality became a vital factor. There is evidence that he had been a headstrong and unruly boy, but he later became concerned only with religious observances and the planning of his educational foundations (Eton College in 1440–41, King's College, Cambridge, in 1441). Home politics were dominated by the rivalries of a series of overpowerful ministers. By early 1449 the contenders for power were the Lancastrian Edmund Beaufort, duke of Somerset, and Richard, duke of York, a cousin of the king whose claim to the throne, by strict primogeniture, was better than Henry's. Meanwhile, the English hold on France was steadily eroded. Despite a truce—as part of which Henry had married Margaret of Anjou, a niece of the French queen—Maine and Normandy were lost and by 1453 so were the remaining English-held lands in Guyenne.

Henry had a period of mental disturbance (July 1453–December 1454), during which York was lord protector, but his hopes of ultimately succeeding Henry were shattered by the birth of Edward, prince of Wales, in 1453. A return to power of Somerset in 1455 made war inevitable, and although he was killed in battle in 1455, Queen Margaret gradually undermined York's ascendancy, and fighting was renewed in 1459. After the Yorkists had captured Henry at Northampton in 1460, it was agreed that Henry should remain king but recognize York, and not his own son Edward, as heir to the throne. York was killed at Wakefield (Dec. 30, 1460), and Henry was recaptured by the Lancastrians in 1461. York's heir, nevertheless, was proclaimed king as Edward IV. Henry fled with his wife and son to Scotland, returning to England in 1464 to support an unsuccessful Lancastrian rising. He was eventually captured (July 1465) in Lancashire and imprisoned in the Tower of London. A quarrel between Edward IV and Richard Neville, earl of Warwick, led Warwick to restore Henry to the throne in October 1470, and Edward fled abroad. But he soon returned, defeated and killed Warwick, and destroyed Queen Margaret's forces at Tewkesbury (May 4, 1471). The death of Prince Edward in that battle sealed Henry's fate, and he was murdered in the Tower of London soon afterward.

the play rapidly shifts between the power struggles at the English court and the war in France. The former spill into the latter when the feuding dukes of York and Somerset quarrel over who is responsible for sending reinforcements to save the noble Lord Talbot. As *Part 1* ends, the Earl of Suffolk, who has persuaded Henry to marry Margaret of Anjou, plans to use the alliance to take power for himself: "Margaret shall now be Queen and rule the King; / But I will rule both her, the King, and realm." His plan's first success comes as *Part 2* begins, when Henry elevates him to the dukedom of Suffolk.

Henry VI, Part 1 covers the early part of King Henry's reign and ends with events immediately preceding the opening of *Part 2*. It contains the entirely nonhistorical scene in which Richard Plantagenet, later duke of York, chooses a white rose and John Beaufort, earl (later duke) of Somerset, a red rose as emblems of their respective houses of York and Lancaster. It is uncertain whether *Part 1* was Shakespeare's first effort at a historical play, written before the other two parts, or a "prequel" that was written subsequently to provide an introduction to the events in *Part 2* and *Part 3*. With the Henry VI trilogy (leading up to the devastating portrayal of evil in *Richard III*), Shakespeare analyzes the harrowing process by which England suffered through decades of civil war until the victory of Henry Tudor (Henry VII) at the Battle of Bosworth Field in 1485.

HENRY VI, PART 2

The version of this play published in the First Folio of 1623 is considerably longer than an earlier corrupt edition and seems to have been based on an authorial manuscript. *Henry VI, Part 2* is the second in the sequence of four history plays treating the Wars of the Roses between the houses of Lancaster and York.

In *Part 2* the factional fighting at court is increased rather than lessened by the arrival of Margaret of Anjou, the new queen, who—together with her lover, the duke of Suffolk—plots against Humphrey, duke of Gloucester, and his ambitious duchess, Eleanor. The power struggle swirls around the saintly, ineffectual King Henry until gradually the dynamic Richard Plantagenet, duke of York, who has pretended to support Margaret while secretly hatching his own plot, emerges as the chief contender for the throne. The commons grow increasingly restive, especially when Duke Humphrey appears to have been murdered by his political enemies. Anarchy reaches its zenith when a Kentishman named Jack Cade, encouraged by Richard Plantagenet, mounts an insurrection that plays havoc in the streets of London until it is finally put down. Open civil war between the Yorkists and the Lancastrians is now imminent.

Portrait of the real Henry VII, who defeated Richard III at the Battle of Bosworth field to begin the reign of the Tudors in England. Apic/ Hulton Fine Art Collection/Getty Images

WARS OF THE ROSES

Both the House of York and the House of Lancaster claimed the throne through descent from the sons of Edward III. Since the Lancastrians had occupied the throne from 1399, the Yorkists might never have pressed a claim but for the near anarchy prevailing in the mid-15th century. After the death of Henry V in 1422 the country was subject to the long and factious minority of Henry VI. Great magnates with private armies dominated the countryside. Lawlessness was rife and taxation burdensome. When he attained his majority, Henry proved ineffectual and subject to spells of madness, and he was dominated by his ambitious queen, Margaret of Anjou, his marriage to whom had been arranged as part of a truce in the Hundred Years' War between France and England.

When Henry lapsed into insanity in 1453, a powerful baronial clique, backed by Richard Neville, the earl of Warwick (the "Kingmaker"), installed Richard, duke of York, as protector of the realm. When Henry recovered in 1455 he reestablished the authority of Margaret's party, forcing York to take up arms for self-protection. The first battle of the wars, at St. Albans (May 22, 1455), resulted in a Yorkist victory and four years of uneasy truce.

Civil war was resumed in 1459. Margaret outlawed the Yorkist leaders, but the king was captured by the Yorkists in July 1460. Margaret refused to accept the compromise by which York was declared the king's successor and her own son disinherited. Her partisans killed York near Wakefield, Yorkshire, in December 1460 and freed the king from captivity at the second Battle of St. Albans in February 1461. But Edward of York, Richard's son, seized the throne as Edward IV on March 4 and crushed Margaret's army at the Battle of Towton, Yorkshire, on March 29. She fled to Scotland with her husband and son. The first major phase of the fighting was over.

The next round of the wars arose out of disputes within the Yorkist ranks. Warwick and his circle were increasingly passed over at Edward's court. More seriously, Warwick differed with the king on foreign policy. In 1469 civil war was renewed. Warwick and Edward's brother George, duke of Clarence, fomented risings in the north. In July they defeated Edward's supporters, afterward holding the king prisoner. By March 1470, however, Edward regained control, forcing Warwick and Clarence to flee to France. There they allied themselves with the French king Louis XI and their former enemy, Margaret of Anjou. In October 1470 Warwick successfully deposed

Edward and restored the crown to Henry VI. Edward fled to the Netherlands with his followers and, securing Burgundian aid, returned to England in March 1471. He outmaneuvered Warwick, regained the loyalty of Clarence, and decisively defeated and killed Warwick at Barnet on April 14. That very day, Margaret had landed at Weymouth. Hearing the news of Barnet, she marched west, trying to reach the safety of Wales; but Edward won the race to the Severn. At Tewkesbury (May 4) Margaret was captured, her forces destroyed, and her son killed. Shortly afterward, Henry VI was murdered in the Tower of London. Edward's throne was secure for the rest of his life (he died in 1483).

In 1483 Edward's brother Richard III, overriding the claims of his nephew, the young Edward V, alienated many Yorkists, who then turned to the last hope of the Lancastrians, Henry Tudor (later Henry VII). With the help of the French and of Yorkist defectors, Henry defeated and killed Richard at Bosworth Field on Aug. 22, 1485, bringing the wars to a close. By his marriage to Edward IV's daughter Elizabeth of York in 1486, Henry united the Yorkist and Lancastrian claims. Henry defeated a Yorkist rising supporting the pretender Lambert Simnel on June 16, 1487, a date which some historians prefer over the traditional 1485 for the termination of the wars.

Artist's depiction of the Battle of Towton during the War of the Roses. Hulton Archive/Getty Images

HENRY VI, PART 3

This play, like *Henry IV, Part 2*, was first published in a corrupt quarto. The version published in the First Folio of 1623 is considerably longer and seems to have been based on an authorial manuscript.

Part 3 begins as the Yorkists seize power and inveigle the inept Henry VI to disinherit his son in favour of the Yorkist claim. Although this arrangement provides for Henry to reign until he dies, the Yorkists soon persuade themselves to violate that treaty and take the throne by force. Open war is the result. Queen Margaret is intent upon gaining the throne for her disinherited son, Edward, prince of Wales. She elicits the aid of Lord Clifford and ultimately defeats York in battle, stabbing him to death while he curses her as "she-wolf of France" and "more inhuman, more inexorable, / Oh, ten times more, than tigers of Hyrcania." As Henry drifts wistfully through the action, lamenting his fate, York's sons consolidate their power. The Lancastrians briefly regain the ascendancy after Edward IV (the eldest of these sons and now king) ignores a proposed marriage to the French princess that has been arranged by the earl of Warwick and King Lewis (Louis) XI of France and instead marries the widowed Elizabeth, Lady Grey. Margaret's triumph is short-lived, however, and the Lancastrians are defeated at the Battle of Tewkesbury. Throughout this period of civil war, Richard, duke of Gloucester, the youngest brother of the new king Edward IV, emerges as a balefully ambitious schemer for power. He begins to reveal the accomplished villain who will emerge full-blown as the title figure in *Richard III*.

RICHARD III

This play was published in 1597 in a quarto edition seemingly reconstructed from memory by the acting company

SHAKESPEARE'S EDWARD III?

The play *Edward III* is sometimes attributed to Shakespeare, though without much evidence other than the resemblances of this play to Shakespeare's early history plays and an occasional passage. It was not included in the First Folio of 1623. A quarto text was published in 1596. The play must have been written prior to that date, presumably in the early 1590s, when history plays of this sort were much in vogue. It was based largely on Holinshed's *Chronicles*.

The play depicts Edward III's great victories in France, especially at Crécy (1346) and Poitiers (1356), during the 14th century. Edward is portrayed as a heroic king, and his son Edward, the Black Prince, is even more stalwart than he. Much of the latter part of the play is devoted to military action in France, some of it near Calais.

The play opens as Edward justifies his wars (historically, the Hundred Years' War, beginning in 1337) on the basis of genealogical claims that sound like those of Henry V for claiming the French kingdom in *Henry V*. The play *Edward III* patriotically defends the English claim. The French and their allies—King John, his sons Charles and Philip, the duke of Lorraine, Lord Villiers, and others—are at times duplicitous and cowardly, though some Frenchmen do keep their word. The Scots are presented in an even more unattractive light; King David II and the Douglases cravenly take advantage of England's preoccupation with France to attack England from the rear. They prove no match for the English, however; Edward is able, at Halidon Hill, to avenge England's terrible loss to the Scots at the infamous Battle of Bannockburn in the time of Edward II (1314), which resulted in Scotland's independence.

An attractive sidelight in the play—unhistorical and so engaging that it is a sentimental favourite among critics to have

Artwork depicting the meeting of Edward III and Philip VI of France during the battle at Crécy. © Everett Collection/SuperStock

been written by Shakespeare—is the wooing by Edward III of the Countess of Salisbury, daughter of the earl of Warwick. Living in the north of England during her husband's absence, the Countess is especially vulnerable to Scottish attacks and plundering across the border, though she shows herself bravely able to fend them off without much help. Edward, coming north to encounter the Scottish invasion, is smitten with the Countess and proposes a relationship that is plainly adulterous, since the Countess's husband is alive and well even if necessarily absent from their home. Worse still, Edward falls so under the tyranny of his passion that he uses his great authority over the earl of Warwick to suggest that he prevail upon his daughter to give in to his constant requests.

Eventually the Countess's own fearless virtue, prompting her to threaten suicide if Edward persists, persuades the king that he has erred egregiously in his pursuit of a married woman, however attractive. He comes to his senses and goes on to become England's great warrior king against the French. The episode illustrates both how mighty men have their failings and how the best of them are able to control their own improper instincts. The political ramifications are telling: A king of England is an absolute monarch whom no one may correct except himself. Edward absorbs this instructive lesson and is much the stronger for having done so.

when a copy of the play was missing. The text in the First Folio of 1623 is substantially better, having been heavily corrected with reference to an independent manuscript. *Richard III* is the last in Shakespeare's first sequence of history plays treating major events of English history during the late 14th and early 15th centuries.

The dissembling and physically deformed Richard, duke of Gloucester, reveals his true purpose in the opening soliloquy of *Richard III*:

> And therefore, since I cannot prove a lover
> To entertain these fair well-spoken days,
> I am determined to prove a villain.

Having killed King Henry VI and Henry's son, the prince of Wales, in *Henry VI, Part 3*, Richard sets out to kill all who stand between him and the throne of England. He woos and marries Lady Anne, whose husband (Edward, prince of Wales) and father-in-law he has murdered, and then arranges for Anne's death as well once she is no

Granite tableau representing Richard III, *adorning a wall of the Folger Shakespeare Library in Washington, D.C.* Library of Congress Prints and Photographs Division

longer useful to him. He displays his animosity toward King Edward's wife and then widow, Queen Elizabeth, by arranging for the deaths of her sons, the Marquess of Dorset and Lord Grey, and her brother, Anthony Woodville, Earl Rivers. He orders the execution of Lord Hastings when that courtier proves loyal to King Edward's children.

At first Richard is ably assisted by the Duke of Buckingham, who readily persuades Cardinal Bourchier to remove the young Duke of York from the protection of sanctuary and place him and his brother under their uncle's "protection" in the Tower. Buckingham further arranges for and later explains away the hurried execution of Hastings, spreads ugly rumours about the bastardy of the young princes and of Edward himself, and stage-manages Richard's apparently reluctant acceptance of the crown. The nefarious partnership between Richard and Buckingham ends when Buckingham balks at killing the young princes and then flees to escape the same fate. An army led by Henry Tudor, earl of Richmond, challenges Richard's claim to the throne. On the night before the Battle of Bosworth Field, Richard is haunted by the ghosts of all whom he has murdered. After a desperate fight, Richard is killed, and Richmond becomes King Henry VII.

KING JOHN

The Life and Death of King John was published in the First Folio of 1623 from an authorial manuscript that may have been copied and supplied with some theatrical touches. The source of the play was a two-part drama generally known as *The Troublesome Raigne of John King of England*. This earlier play, first printed in 1591, was based on the chronicles of Raphael Holinshed and Edward Hall. Shakespeare also consulted some chronicle materials, as well as John Foxe's *Acts and Monuments* (1563), known as *The Book of Martyrs*. Shakespeare made few changes to the plot in his version, but the dialogue and insights about the characters are all his own.

The title figure provides the central focus of the play and is surrounded by many contrasting characters—each able to influence him and bringing irresolvable and individual problems into dramatic focus. Chief among these characters are John's domineering mother, Queen Eleanor (formerly Eleanor of Aquitaine), and Philip the Bastard, who supports the king and yet mocks all political and moral pretensions.

THE REAL RICHARD III

(b. Oct. 2, 1452, Fotheringhay Castle,
Northamptonshire, Eng.—d. Aug. 22, 1485,
near Market Bosworth, Leicestershire)

Richard was the youngest son of Richard, duke of York, and was made duke of Gloucester in 1461 after his eldest brother had deposed Henry VI and assumed power as Edward IV. Briefly driven into exile, Edward and Richard returned to England in March 1471, and Richard commanded the vanguard forces in two victories over the Lancastrians that led to Edward's restoration. As a reward for his fidelity, the king gave him high offices and large grants of land.

Upon the death of his brother the king, in 1483, Richard became protector of the realm for Edward's son and successor, the 12-year-old king Edward V. But he soon came into conflict with Edward IV's widow, Elizabeth Woodville, and her faction. Richard broke the power of the Woodvilles by arresting and eventually executing their leaders and by taking into custody Edward V and his nine-year-old brother. London preachers were then persuaded to announce that Edward IV's marriage had been invalid and his children illegitimate, and that Richard was therefore his brother's rightful successor. These claims were endorsed by an assembly of lords and commoners, and Richard III officially began his reign.

When the two young princes disappeared in August 1483, it was widely rumoured that Richard, their uncle, had had them murdered. A rebellion raised in southern England by Richard's once-close associate Henry Stafford, duke of Buckingham, in October 1483 quickly collapsed, and Stafford was executed. But the defection reduced still further the unsure foundation of Richard's power. Richard then began to devote his full attention to his kingly duties. He promoted trade and instituted financial reforms. But time was not on his side, as those whose support he desperately needed found it difficult to accept him as a legitimate ruler.

Meanwhile, Richard's enemies were joining his rival, Henry Tudor, earl of Richmond, a Lancastrian claimant to the throne living in exile in France. In August 1485 Henry and his army engaged Richard in battle on Bosworth Field. Richard's forces were larger than Henry's, but several of the king's most powerful nobles defected at a crucial moment in the battle. Refusing to flee, Richard died fighting bravely. Though he was vilified for centuries, Richard is regarded by modern scholars as a potentially capable monarch whose reputation for wickedness originated in 16th-century political propaganda.

As the play begins, King John, with the aid of his mother, has usurped the royal title of his nephew Arthur; the king of France, on threat of war, has demanded that Arthur be placed on the throne. Two brothers, Philip and Robert Faulconbridge, enter arguing over their inheritance. Eleanor recognizes the resemblance between Philip and her late son King Richard Coeur-de-lion. After Philip agrees to drop all claim to the Faulconbridge lands, his mother admits that he is indeed Richard's son. Thereafter, the Bastard, newly knighted as Sir Richard Plantagenet, becomes John's staunchest military commander in the war against France.

As the fighting rages on, a compromise is arranged in which Lewis, the dauphin, heir to the French throne, marries John's niece Blanche. This expediency fails to end the war, however, with armies led by Eleanor and Arthur's combatant mother, Constance, at the forefront. An English victory delivers young Arthur into the hands of

A scene from a 1957 production of The Life and Death of King John in Stratford-upon-Avon. The obstacle-filled life and reign of the real King John provided great fodder for the playwright. Central Press/ Hulton Archive/Getty Images

King John. This success soon turns against John, however, when he finds that Arthur is too dangerous a presence because he has become a rallying point for John's political enemies. John orders Hubert de Burgh to kill the captive Arthur. After Hubert finds that he cannot carry out such an inhumane command and allows the child to survive, Arthur dies in a tragic fall while trying to escape.

Cardinal Pandulph, having urged the French to support the papacy against the rebellious John, succeeds in

THE REAL KING JOHN

(b. Dec. 24, 1167, Oxford—d. Oct. 18/19, 1216,
Newark, Nottinghamshire, Eng.)

John was the youngest son of Henry II and Eleanor of Aquitaine. Henry's plan (1173) to assign to John, his favourite son (whom he had nicknamed Lackland), extensive lands upon his marriage was defeated by the rebellion the proposal provoked among John's elder brothers. Henry's continued favour to him contributed to the rebellion of his eldest surviving son, Richard I (later called the Lion-heart), in June 1189. For obscure reasons John deserted Henry for Richard.

On Richard's accession in July 1189, John received several favours but soon Richard recognized his nephew, the three-year-old Arthur I, duke of Brittany, the son of his deceased elder brother Geoffrey, as his heir to the throne. From 1196 Arthur was reared in the household of Philip II of France, causing Richard to disinherit the boy in favour of John. After Richard's sudden death in 1199, John was accepted as king in England and Normandy. Philip, however, recognized Arthur's right to Brittany, Anjou, Aquitaine, and Maine and betrothed his daughter Mary to the young duke. The situation was complicated by Eleanor of Aquitaine, widow of Henry II, who wanted Aquitaine and Anjou for John. In 1202 Arthur was captured in battle by John and imprisoned. According to tradition, he was murdered either by John himself or at his order.

The renewal of war in France was triggered by John's second marriage (his first was dissolved). In the conflict provoked by his marriage to Isabella, the heiress to Angoulême, he lost Normandy, then Anjou, Maine, and parts of Poitou. These failures were a damaging blow to John's prestige. His determination to reverse the continental failure bore fruit in ruthlessly efficient financial administration and a series of measures that provided the material basis for the charges of tyranny later brought against him.

John next attempted to gain control of the papacy, and, though he eventually submitted, his treatment of the church during his 5-year excommunication angered monastic chroniclers, who henceforth loaded him with charges of tyranny, cruelty, and, less reasonably, of sacrilege and irreligion. Further, recurrent baronial discontent came to a head. After his defeat in a long-planned campaign against the French and the outbreak of civil war at home, John was forced to accept the baronial terms embodied in a document known as the Magna Carta, which ensured feudal rights and restated English law.

encouraging a French invasion of England, only to discover, when John has reluctantly submitted to the papacy, that the French dauphin will not call off his invading forces. The war thus becomes an exercise in futility on all sides. Increasingly weak and uncertain, John grows ill. Only the Bastard fights on until news comes that John has been poisoned by a traitorous monk. After Prince Henry arrives to care for his dying father and accept his imminent accession to the throne, the Bastard at last accepts that peace is at hand and pledges fealty to the new king.

Chapter 3

COMPLETION OF THE HISTORIES

C oncurrent with his writing of his fine romantic com-edies, Shakespeare also brought to completion (for the time being, at least) his project of writing 15th-century English history. Having finished in 1589–94 the tetralogy about Henry VI, Edward IV, and Richard III (bringing the story to 1485) and then about 1594–96 writing his play about the 13th-century King John, Shakespeare turned to the late 14th and early 15th centuries and to the chronicle of Richard II, Henry IV, and Henry's legendary son Henry V. This inversion of historical order in the two tetralogies allowed Shakespeare to finish his sweep of late medieval English history with Henry V, a hero king in a way that Richard III could never pretend to be.

Richard II (c. 1595–96), written throughout in blank verse, is a sombre play about political impasse. It contains almost no humour, other than a wry scene in which the new king, Henry IV, must adjudicate the competing claims of the Duke of York and his Duchess, the first of whom wishes to see his son Aumerle executed for treason and the second of whom begs for mercy. Henry is able to be merciful on this occasion, since he has now won the kingship, and thus gives to this scene an upbeat movement. Earlier, however, the mood is grim. Richard, installed at an early age into the kingship, proves irresponsible as a ruler. He unfairly banishes his own first cousin, Henry Bolingbroke (later

THE HISTORIES OF EDWARD HALL AND RAPHAEL HOLINSHED

The two sources to which Shakespeare (and indeed many other dramatists) turned most often for English history were histories written by Edward Hall (1497–1547) and Raphael Holinshed (d. c. 1580). Hall's work, *The Union of the Two Noble and Illustrate Famelies of Lancastre and Yorke* (1548; 2nd ed., 1550), left unfinished at his death, is of considerable value for the contemporary reign of Henry VIII, and its literary quality is higher than that of most chronicles of the time. In it and in the second edition of Holinshed's *Chronicles*, Shakespeare found material for *Macbeth*, *King Lear*, and *Cymbeline*, as well as many of his historical plays.

Edward Hall (or Halle) was educated at Eton and at King's College, Cambridge (B.A., 1518). He had entered Grey's Inn by 1521, and thereafter he earned a living as a lawyer. Hall became common sergeant of London in 1533 and undersheriff in 1535. He was also a member of Parliament for Much Wenlock (1529) and Bridgnorth (1542) in Shropshire. Hall's *Chronicle* covers the reigns of English kings from Henry IV to the death of Henry VIII. In his will Hall bequeathed his work, finished through the "four and twenty year of Henry the Eight," to the historian and printer Richard Grafton, who published it.

From roughly 1560 Raphael Holinshed lived in London, where he was employed as a translator by the Dutch-born printer Reginald (or Reyner) Wolfe, who was preparing a universal history. After Wolfe's death in 1573 the scope of the work was abridged, and it appeared, with many illustrations, as the *Chronicles of England, Scotlande, and Irelande*, 2 vol. (dated 1577).

The *Chronicles* was compiled largely uncritically from many sources of varying degrees of trustworthiness. The texts of the first and second (1587) editions were expurgated by order of the Privy Council, and the excisions from the second edition were published separately in 1723. An edition of the complete, unexpurgated text of 1587, edited by Henry Ellis and titled *Holinshed's Chronicles of England, Scotland, and Ireland*, was published in six volumes (1807–08, reissued 1976). Several selections have also appeared, including *Holinshed's Chronicle as Used in Shakespeare's Plays*, edited by Allardyce and Josephine Nicoll (1927); *Shakespeare's Holinshed*, compiled and edited by Richard Hosley (1968); and *The Peaceable and Prosperous Regiment of Blessed Queene Elisabeth: A Facsimile from Holinshed's Chronicles (1587)*, edited by Cyndia Susan Clegg, with textual commentary by Randall McLeod (2005).

to be Henry IV), whereas the king himself appears to be guilty of ordering the murder of an uncle. When Richard keeps the dukedom of Lancaster from Bolingbroke without proper legal authority, he manages to alienate many nobles and to encourage Bolingbroke's return from exile. That return, too, is illegal, but it is a fact, and, when several of the nobles (including York) come over to Bolingbroke's side, Richard is forced to abdicate. The rights and wrongs of this power struggle are masterfully ambiguous. History proceeds without any sense of moral imperative. Henry IV is a more capable ruler, but his authority is tarnished by his crimes (including his seeming assent to the execution of Richard), and his own rebellion appears to teach the barons to rebel against him in turn. Henry eventually dies a disappointed man.

The dying king Henry IV must turn royal authority over to young Hal, or Henry, now Henry V. The prospect is dismal both to the dying king and to the members of his court, for Prince Hal has distinguished himself to this point mainly by his penchant for keeping company with the disreputable if engaging Falstaff. The son's attempts at reconciliation with the father succeed temporarily, especially when Hal saves his father's life at the battle of Shrewsbury, but (especially in *Henry IV, Part 2*) his reputation as wastrel will not leave him. Everyone expects from him a reign of irresponsible license, with Falstaff in an influential position. It is for these reasons that the young king must publicly repudiate his old companion of the tavern and the highway, however much that repudiation tugs at his heart and the audience's. Falstaff, for all his debauchery and irresponsibility, is infectiously amusing and delightful. He represents in Hal a spirit of youthful vitality that is left behind only with the greatest of regret as the young man assumes manhood and the role of crown prince. Hal manages all this with aplomb and goes on to defeat the French mightily at the Battle of Agincourt. Even his high jinks are a part of what is so attractive in him. Maturity and position come at a great personal cost: Hal becomes less a frail human being and more the figure of royal authority.

Thus, in his plays of the 1590s, the young Shakespeare concentrated to a remarkable extent on romantic comedies and English history plays. The two genres are nicely complementary: the one deals with courtship and marriage, while the other examines the career of a young man growing up to be a worthy king. Only at the end of the history plays does Henry V have any kind of romantic relationship with a woman, and this one instance is quite unlike courtships in the romantic comedies: Hal is given the Princess of France as his prize, his reward for sturdy manhood. He takes the lead in the wooing scene in which he invites her to join him in a political marriage. In both romantic comedies and English history plays, a young man successfully negotiates the hazardous and potentially rewarding paths of sexual and social maturation.

RICHARD II

This was published in a quarto edition in 1597 and in the First Folio of 1623. The quarto edition omits the deposition scene in Act IV, almost certainly as a result of censorship. The play is the first in a sequence of four history plays (the other three being *Henry IV, Part 1*, *Henry IV, Part 2*, and *Henry V*) known collectively as the "second tetralogy." The story of Richard II was taken mainly from Holinshed's *Chronicles*. While much of the play is true to the facts of Richard's life, Shakespeare's account of his murder rests on no reliable authority.

Richard begins the play as an extravagant, self-indulgent king. He exiles two feuding noblemen, Thomas Mowbray and Henry Bolingbroke, seemingly because Mowbray has been implicated along with Richard himself in the murder of Richard's uncle Thomas of Woodstock, duke of Gloucester, while Bolingbroke, Richard's first cousin, is a threat to the king because he is intent on avenging the death of Gloucester. When John of Gaunt, Bolingbroke's father, dies, Richard seizes his properties to finance a war against the Irish. The seizure gives Bolingbroke an excuse to invade England with his own armies. He insists that his return in arms is solely to regain his illegally seized dukedom. Powerful earls, especially the Earl of Northumberland and his family, support Bolingbroke because of their intense disapproval of Richard's invasion of baronial rights. Richard's last surviving uncle, Edmund of Langley, duke of York, serves as regent while the king is fighting in Ireland. York, however, recognizes that change is inevitable and swears allegiance

Actors (left to right) *Sean McNally, Jolly Abraham, and Grant Goodman, of New York City's Pearl Theatre Company, performing in a 2011 production of* Richard II. © AP Images

to Bolingbroke. York's son, the Duke of Aumerle, remains loyal to Richard despite his father's change of allegiance.

Unable to defeat Bolingbroke militarily, Richard reluctantly agrees to surrender and abdicate the throne. In prison—lonely, miserable, and forgotten—he soliloquizes on the meaning of his suffering. From this moment of truth, he rediscovers pride, trust, and courage, so that, when he is murdered, he dies with access to strength and an ascending spirit. Bolingbroke, now King Henry IV, performs his first royal act (and displays his pragmatic approach to governing) by acquiescing to the Duchess of York's pleas for Aumerle's life while the zealous York demands his "disloyal" son's execution. The play ends with Henry inquiring about his own wastrel son, Prince Hal,

THE REAL RICHARD II

(b. Jan. 6, 1367, Bordeaux [now in France]—d. February 1400, Pontefract, Yorkshire [now in West Yorkshire], England)

Richard was the younger and only surviving son of Edward, the Black Prince, and his wife, Joan of Kent. Because his father died prematurely in 1376, the 11-year-old Richard succeeded his grandfather Edward III as king in June 1377.

Three years later he helped to quell the Peasants' Revolt, a march on London initiated by popular anger over the passage of a poll tax (i.e., a tax paid by every individual regardless of income). Richard helped to end the revolt, but the promises of fiscal reform that he made were soon forgotten. As he gained his majority, Richard began to assert himself. He gathered about him a group of friends and counselors of his own choosing. A struggle for power ensued, eventually leading to the so-called Merciless Parliament, which exiled or executed many of the king's friends.

In a five-year period beginning in 1389, Richard went some way toward attempting to govern well. Taxes fell sharply following a truce with the French in 1389, and from 1389 to 1391 no demands for a tax on "moveable" property were made. Richard also showed greater prudence in rewarding a wider circle of the powerful. Yet the seeming moderation of Richard's rule was matched by a strong emphasis on the reassertion of royal authority. In the 1390s he developed a program to strengthen the material foundations of his rule. He also elaborated the ceremony and protocol of his court.

The highly assertive nature of his kingship revealed itself in his first expedition to Ireland. In 1394–95 he led a substantial force there to buttress the position of the English administration. The native Irish were overawed by the presence of an English king, and the local chieftains, or "High Kings," all attended the court in Dublin to submit to his authority. In letters of submission made for the penitent chieftains, Richard articulated his political vision. Rebellion and disobedience were to be rewarded with appropriate punishment, the rebel Irish were to enter into the king's obedience, and all Irish, of whatever status, were to perform their accustomed obligations to him.

The exalted notions that Richard articulated in Ireland formed the background for his dramatic reassertion of royal authority two years later in England. In 1397 he began to imprison, exile, and execute his enemies and to seize their property. Among those exiled was his cousin Henry Bolingbroke, son of John of Gaunt, duke of Lancaster.

In 1399, when John of Gaunt died, Richard seized the Lancastrian estates. But Bolingbroke returned to England with a few followers to recover his vast properties. Thousands of Englishmen joined his army. Richard had gone to Ireland again to put down a rebellion. When he landed in Wales, many of the soldiers who had accompanied him deserted. Helpless, he surrendered to Henry and promised to give up his throne if his life was spared. Parliament accepted his abdication and conferred the crown on Henry, who as Henry IV was the first Lancastrian king. Richard was imprisoned. The next year, after a rebellion had broken out in his favour, he was reported dead.

and swearing to make a pilgrimage to the Holy Land to atone for his part in Richard's murder.

HENRY IV, PART 1

Henry IV, Part 1 was published from a reliable authorial draft in a 1598 quarto edition. It was the second play of the second tetralogy. The historical facts in the play were taken primarily from Holinshed's *Chronicles*, but Sir John Falstaff and his Eastcheap cronies are original creations (with some indebtedness to popular traditions about Prince Hal's prodigal, or misspent, youth that had been incorporated into a play of the 1580s called *The Famous Victories of Henry the Fifth*) who add an element of robust comedy to *Henry IV* that is missing in Shakespeare's earlier chronicles.

Set in a kingdom plagued with rebellion, treachery, and shifting alliances in the period following the deposition of King Richard II, the two parts of *Henry IV* focus especially on the development of Prince Hal (later Henry V) from wastrel to ruler rather than on the title character. Indeed, the king is often overshadowed not only by his son but also by Hotspur, the young rebel military leader, and by Hal's roguish companion Falstaff. Secondary characters (many of them comic) are numerous. The plot shifts rapidly between scenes of raucous comedy and the war against the alliance of the Welsh and the rebellious Percy family of Northumberland.

As *Part 1* begins, Henry IV, wearied from the strife that has accompanied his accession to the throne, is renewing his earlier vow to make a pilgrimage to the Holy Land. He learns that Owen Glendower, the Welsh chieftain, has captured Edmund Mortimer, the earl of March, and that Henry Percy, known as Hotspur, son of the earl of Northumberland, has refused to release his Scottish prisoners until the king has ransomed Mortimer. Henry laments that his own son is not like the fearless Hotspur. As the war escalates, Glendower, Mortimer (now married to Glendower's daughter), and Hotspur (now allied with the Welsh) conspire to divide Henry's kingdom into three equal parts.

Meanwhile, Prince Hal and his cronies, including the fat, boisterous Falstaff and his red-nosed sidekick,

FALSTAFF

Sir John Falstaff, who appears in four of Shakespeare's plays, is one of the most famous comic characters in all English literature. Entirely the creation of Shakespeare, Falstaff is said to have been partly modeled on Sir John Oldcastle, a soldier and the martyred leader of the Lollard sect. Indeed, Shakespeare had originally called this character Sir John Oldcastle in the first version of *Henry IV, Part 1,* but had changed the name before the play was registered, doubtless because descendants of the historical Oldcastle—who were then prominent at court—protested. He chose the name Falstaff partly because it contained echoes of the name Sir John Fastolf, which he had earlier given to a cowardly knight in *Henry VI, Part 1.* (The historical Sir John Fastolf was a career soldier who in the second phase of the Hundred Years' War had something of a reputation as a coward; however, Shakespeare's presentation of his character was libelous.)

In *Henry IV, Part 1*, Falstaff is a boon companion to the young Prince Hal, a type of nonjudgmental father-substitute he calls that "reverend vice...that father ruffian, that vanity of years" (and, in Falstaff's own imagination, that "kind Jack Falstaff, true Jack Falstaff, valiant Jack Falstaff"), and throughout the play Falstaff comments on the political machinations with inglorious, reckless, egotistical good sense.

In *Henry IV, Part 2,* Falstaff and his disreputable crew are rejected by Henry V when the former profligate prince assumes the dignities of the crown. Falstaff's death is movingly reported in *Henry V*, but he makes another appearance in *The Merry Wives of Windsor,* a play that, according to (largely unsupported) tradition, was written at the express command of Queen Elizabeth I, who had wished to see Falstaff in love. This play's Falstaff, now reduced to an opportunistic and comically unsuccessful seducer, was the subject of Giuseppe Verdi's opera *Falstaff* (produced 1893) and Otto Nicolai's *Die lustigen Weiber von Windsor* (produced 1849).

Bardolph, have been drinking and playing childish pranks at Mistress Quickly's inn at Eastcheap. Hal, who admits in an aside that he is associating with these thieving rogues only temporarily, nevertheless agrees to take part with them in an actual highway robbery. He does so under certain conditions: the money is to be taken away from Falstaff and his companions by Prince Hal and his comrade Poins in disguise, and the money is then to be returned to its rightful owners, so that the whole caper is a practical joke on Falstaff rather than a robbery.

This merriment is interrupted by Hal's being called to his father's aid in the war against the Welsh and the Percys. Hal and his father manage to make up their differences, at least for a time, most of all when Hal saves the life of his father in combat. Hal further proves his valour in battle, where he chides Falstaff for malingering and drunkenness and then kills Hotspur in personal combat during the Battle of Shrewsbury. Hal laments the wasteful death of his noble opponent and of Falstaff, on the ground nearby. But Falstaff was only feigning death, and, when he claims to have killed Hotspur, Hal agrees to support the lie. At the play's end, rebellion has been only temporarily defeated.

HENRY IV, PART 2

The third part of Shakespeare's second history tetralogy, *Henry IV, Part 2*, was published in a corrupt text based in part on memorial reconstruction in a quarto edition in 1600. A better text, printed in the main from an authorial manuscript, appeared in the First Folio of 1623 and is generally the more reliable version. The historical facts of the play were taken primarily from Holinshed's *Chronicles*, but Shakespeare's comic secondary characters,

Shown in a 2005 performance of Shakespeare's Henry IV, Part 1 are Matthew MacFayden (seated) as Prince Hal and Michael Gambon as Falstaff, at the Royal National Theatre in London. Elliot Franks/ WireImage/Getty Images

including Falstaff, were highly successful inventions of the playwright. In *Henry IV, Part 2* these Eastcheap figures dominate the action even more than they do in *Part 1*.

Henry IV's son John of Lancaster is leading the ongoing war against the Welsh chieftain, Owen Glendower, and Hotspur's father, Henry Percy, earl of Northumberland. The swaggering Falstaff has become even more corpulent and outrageous, sponging off his hostess, Mistress Quickly, abusing the Lord Chief Justice, preening for the admiring Doll Tearsheet, and taking advantage of everyone, especially his ensign, Pistol, and his old friends Justice Shallow and Justice Silence.

Prince Hal, worried about his father's ill health but still curious about Falstaff's activities, goes to Eastcheap in disguise to spy on his old friends. When the king learns of Hal's whereabouts, he despairs for the future. News comes that Prince John has settled the war (through a perfidious betrayal of promises made to the enemy leaders as a condition of their disbanding their forces). Henry talks, yet again, about a pilgrimage so that he can die in the Holy Land. After a misunderstanding in which Hal—thinking his father has died—removes the crown from the king's pillow and leaves the sickroom, father and son are reconciled on the king's deathbed. The wily Henry advises Hal to avoid internal strife during his own reign by seeking foreign quarrels.

Hal prepares to become king, setting aside his previous frivolous image and reassuring his brothers of his loyalty to them and his genuine grief at their mutual loss. Falstaff arrives with his entourage, expecting a lively and generous welcome from his old friend. Instead, Hal, now King Henry V, denounces Falstaff, orders him and his cronies to repent their profligate ways, and has the Lord Chief Justice take them to the Fleet prison until they have

Richard Burton (right) *as Prince Hal, holding the crown he has removed from the head of his dying father, King Henry IV (Harry Andrews) in* Henry IV, Part 2, *staged in Stratford-upon-Avon in 1951.* Popperfoto/Getty Images

reformed. As they are led away, Prince John prophesies war with France.

HENRY V

Shakespeare's *Henry V* was first performed in 1599 and published in 1600 in a corrupt quarto edition. The text in the First Folio of 1623, printed seemingly from an

THE REAL HENRY IV

(b. April? 1366, Bolingbroke Castle, Lincolnshire,
England—d. March 20, 1413, London)

Henry was the eldest surviving son of John of Gaunt, duke of Lancaster, by his first wife, Blanche. Before becoming king, he was known as Henry Bolingbroke. He first entered politics in 1386 as an opponent of the crown. In 1387–89, with Thomas Mowbray (later 1st duke of Norfolk) and others, he outlawed Richard's closest associates and forced the king to submit. It was a circumstance Richard never forgave. Bolingbroke went on Crusade into Lithuania (1390) and Prussia (1392). In 1398 Bolingbroke was banished. When John of Gaunt died in 1399 and the crown seized his lands, Bolingbroke invaded England, forced Richard's surrender and abdication, and was crowned King Henry IV on Sept. 30, 1399.

During the first five years of his reign, Henry was attacked by a formidable array of domestic and foreign enemies. He quashed a conspiracy of Richard's supporters in January 1400. Eight months later the Welsh landowner Owen Glendower raised a rebellion against English rule in Wales. Henry led a number of fruitless expeditions into Wales from 1400 to 1405, but his son, Prince Henry (later Henry V), had greater success in reasserting royal control over the region. Meanwhile, Glendower allied with the powerful Percy family—Henry Percy, earl of Northumberland, and his son Sir Henry Percy, called Hotspur. Hotspur's brief uprising was the most serious challenge faced by Henry during his reign, but the king's forces killed the rebel in battle near Shrewsbury, Shropshire, in July 1403. Though the worst of his troubles were over, Henry continued to face foreign and domestic threats throughout the remainder of his life. As Henry's health deteriorated, a power struggle developed within his administration between his favourite, Thomas Arundel, archbishop of Canterbury, and a faction headed by Henry's half brothers and Prince Henry. Tension between father and son was high when Henry became totally incapacitated late in 1412. Henry died in Westminster Abbey, after a five-year illness.

authorial manuscript, is substantially longer and more reliable. *Henry V* is the fourth and last play of the second tetralogy, treating major events in English history of the late 14th and early 15th centuries. As in the first three, the main source of the play was Holinshed's *Chronicles*, but Shakespeare may also have been influenced by an earlier play about King Henry V called *The Famous Victories of Henry the Fifth.*

In keeping with his father's advice in the preceding play (*Henry IV, Part 2*) to seek foreign quarrels, Henry V, resolves to subjugate France and retake the lands in France previously held by England. His political and military advisers conclude that he has a rightful claim to the French crown and encourage him to follow the military exploits of his royal ancestors. The action of the play culminates in Henry's campaign in France with a ragtag army. The depiction of the character of Henry dominates the play throughout, from his nervous watch before the Battle of Agincourt, when he walks disguised among his fearful soldiers and prays for victory, to his courtship of Princess Katharine, which is romantic and tender despite the marriage's having been arranged by the duke of Burgundy.

Although almost all the fighting occurs offstage, the recruits, professional soldiers, dukes, and princes are shown preparing for defeat or victory. Comic figures abound, notably the Welsh captain, Fluellen, and some of

Actor Jamie Parker (centre) *as Henry V preparing to lead his motley crew of soldiers into battle in a scene from a 2012 production of Shakespeare's* Henry V *at the reconstructed Globe Theatre in London.* © AP Images

Henry's former companions, notably Nym, Bardolph, and Pistol, who is now married to Mistress Quickly. Falstaff, however, dies offstage, perhaps because Shakespeare felt his boisterous presence would detract from the more serious themes of the play.

Shakespeare hedges the patriotic fantasy of English greatness in *Henry V* with hesitations and qualifications

THE REAL HENRY V

(b. Sept. 16?, 1387, Monmouth,
Monmouthshire, Wales—d. Aug. 31, 1422, Bois
de Vincennes, Fr.)

Henry was the eldest son of Henry, earl of Derby (afterward Henry IV), by Mary de Bohun. When he was only 16 years old he was in command of the English forces that defeated the Percys and Neville at Shrewsbury. He helped put down the Welsh revolt, and in 1411 he led an expedition to France. His father's long illness brought him heavy political responsibilities. Despite his early entry into public life, he was well educated by the standards of his time. He grew up fond of music and reading and became the first English king who could both read and write with ease in the vernacular tongue. The stories of Prince Henry's reckless and dissolute youth, immortalized by Shakespeare, and of the sudden change that overtook him when he became king, have been traced back to within 20 years of his death and cannot be dismissed as pure fabrication.

Henry succeeded his father in 1413. He put forth again the claim to the French throne originally raised by Edward III. Not content with a demand for possession of Aquitaine and other lands ceded by the French at the Treaty of Calais (1360), he also laid claim to Normandy, Touraine, and Maine (the former Angevin holdings) and to parts of France that had never been in English hands.

Henry V's first campaign brought the capture of Harfleur (September 1415) and the great victory of Agincourt (Oct. 25, 1415). This resounding triumph made Henry the diplomatic arbiter of Europe. After 1417 he returned to the long, grim war of sieges and the gradual conquest of Normandy. Rouen, the capital of northern France, surrendered in January 1419, and the murder of Duke John of Burgundy in September 1419 brought him the Burgundian alliance. These successes forced the French to agree to the Treaty of Troyes on May 21, 1420. Henry was recognized as heir to the French throne and regent of France, and Catherine of Valois, the daughter of Charles, was married to him on June 2. He was now at the height of his power: but his triumph was short-lived. His health grew worse at the sieges of Melun and Meaux, and he died of camp fever at the château of Vincennes in 1422.

about the validity of the myth of glorious nationhood offered by the Agincourt story. The king's speech to his troops before battle on St. Crispin's Day is particularly famous for its evocation of a brotherhood in arms, but Shakespeare has placed it in a context full of ironies and challenging contrasts. In the end the chorus reminds the audience that England was to be plunged into civil war during the reign of Henry V's son, Henry VI.

HENRY VIII

Shakespeare's *Henry VIII* was produced in 1613 and published in the First Folio of 1623 from a transcript of an authorial manuscript.

As the play opens, the duke of Buckingham, having denounced Cardinal Wolsey, lord chancellor to King Henry VIII, for corruption and treason, is himself arrested, along with his son-in-law, Lord Abergavenny. Despite the king's reservations and Queen Katharine's entreaties for justice and truth, Buckingham is convicted as a traitor on the basis of the false testimony of a dismissed servant.

William Terriss as the title character in Henry VIII, *photogravure, 1892.* © Photos.com/Thinkstock

THE REAL HENRY VIII

(b. June 28, 1491, Greenwich, near London,
Eng.—d. Jan. 28, 1547, London)

Henry was the second son of Henry VII, first of the Tudor line, and Elizabeth, daughter of Edward IV, first king of the short-lived line of York. When his elder brother, Arthur, died in 1502, Henry became the heir to the throne. He was a gifted scholar, linguist, composer, and musician. When in 1509 he ascended the throne, great things were expected of him. Six feet tall, powerfully built, and a tireless athlete, huntsman, and dancer, he promised England the joys of spring after the long winter of Henry VII's reign.

Soon after his accession, Henry married Catherine of Aragon, Arthur's widow. He also determined to engage in military adventure, though he himself had no military talent. In Thomas Wolsey, who organized his first campaign in France, Henry discovered his first outstanding minister. By 1515 Wolsey was archbishop of York, lord chancellor of England, and a cardinal of the church. More important, he was the king's good friend, to whom was gladly left the active conduct of affairs, at least for the first 20 years of Henry's reign.

By 1527 Henry had made up his mind to shed his wife. The only one of Catherine's six children who survived infancy was a sickly girl, Princess Mary, and female succession was still doubtful. He wanted a male heir. Then, too, Henry had fallen in love with a lady of the court, Anne Boleyn. It took him six years to marry her. When the pope (Clement VII) would not annul his marriage to Catherine, Henry turned against Wolsey, deprived him of his office of chancellor, and had him arrested on a charge of treason. He then obtained a divorce through Thomas Cranmer, whom he had made archbishop of

Canterbury, and it was soon announced that he had married Anne Boleyn.

The pope was thus defied. All ties that bound the English church to Rome were broken. Appeals to the pope's court were forbidden, all payments to Rome were stopped, and the pope's authority in England was abolished. In 1534 the Act of Supremacy declared Henry himself to be Supreme Head of the Church of England, and anyone who denied this title was guilty of an act of treason. The monasteries throughout England were dissolved and their vast lands and goods turned over to the king, who in turn granted those estates to noblemen who would support his policies.

The king now embarked on the series of matrimonial adventures that made him appear both a monster and a laughingstock. He soon tired of Anne, who failed to produce a male heir. In 1536 she was executed, with other members of the court, for alleged treasonable adultery. Catherine of Aragon, rejected but unbowed, had died a little earlier. Henry immediately married Jane Seymour, who bore his son Edward but died in childbirth (1537). The next three years were filled with attempts to replace her, and the bride chosen was Anne, sister of the duke of Cleves, a pawn in Henry's political strategy. But Henry hated the first sight of her and at once demanded his freedom, an end achieved by a quick divorce.

In 1540–42 he briefly renewed his youth in marriage to the 20-year-old Catherine Howard, whose folly in continuing her promiscuity, even as queen, brought her to the block. The blow finished Henry. Thereafter, he was really a sad and bitter old man, and, though he married once more, to find a measure of peace with the calm and obedient Catherine Parr, his physical ruin was complete.

During Henry's reign the union of England and Wales was completed (1536). Ireland was made a kingdom (1541), and Henry became king of Ireland. His wars with Scotland

and France remained indecisive in spite of some shallow victories. Somewhat ironically, though he himself opposed the Reformation, his creation of a national church marked the real beginning of the English Reformation.

As he is taken away for execution, Buckingham conveys a prophetic warning to beware of false friends.

Henry becomes enamoured of the beautiful Anne Bullen (Boleyn) and, concerned over his lack of a male heir, expresses doubts about the validity of his marriage to Katharine, his brother's widow. Separately, Anne, though reluctant to supplant the queen, accepts the king's proposal. Wolsey tries to extend his power over the king by preventing this marriage, but the lord chancellor's machinations and long-time corruption are finally revealed to all. As he leaves the court, Wolsey encourages his servant Thomas Cromwell to offer his services to Henry, who soon promotes Cromwell to high office. Anne is married to Henry in secret and with great pomp is crowned queen. Although Katharine maintains her dignity throughout her divorce trial and subsequent exile from court, her goodness has no power in the face of political intrigues. She dies, soon after hearing that Wolsey has died repenting for his sins.

The new lord chancellor and other court officials attempt to reassert control over the king by accusing Thomas Cranmer, Henry's loyal archbishop of Canterbury, of heresy. The king is no longer so easily manipulated, however, and Cranmer reveals to the plotters a ring he holds as a mark of the king's favour. Henry further asks Cranmer to baptize his newborn daughter, and the play ends with a final celebration and Cranmer's prophecy of England's glory under the future Queen Elizabeth I.

Henry VIII, which is widely thought to be Shakespeare's last completed play, has had a long and interesting stage history, but since the mid-19th century a number of critics have doubted that Shakespeare was its sole author. Many scenes and splendid speeches were written in a style very similar to that of John Fletcher.

Chapter 4

THE POEMS

Like English prose, English poetry burst into sudden glory in the late 1570s. A decisive shift of taste toward a fluent artistry self-consciously displaying its own grace and sophistication was announced in the works of Edmund Spenser and Sir Philip Sidney. It was accompanied by an upsurge in literary production that came to fruition in the 1590s and 1600s, two decades of astonishing productivity by writers of every persuasion and calibre.

The groundwork was laid in the 30 years from 1550, a period of slowly increasing confidence in the literary competence of the language and tremendous advances in education, which for the first time produced a substantial English readership, keen for literature and possessing cultivated tastes. This development was underpinned by the technological maturity and accelerating output (mainly in pious or technical subjects) of Elizabethan printing. The Stationers' Company, which controlled the publication of books, was incorporated in 1557, and Richard Tottel's *Miscellany* (1557) revolutionized the relationship of poet and audience by making publicly available lyric poetry, which hitherto had circulated only among a close circle of courtly associates. Spenser was the first significant English poet deliberately to use print to advertise his talents.

HENRY WRIOTHESLEY, 3RD EARL OF SOUTHAMPTON

(b. Oct. 6, 1573, Cowdray, Sussex, England—d. Nov. 10, 1624, Bergen op Zoom, Netherlands)

Henry Wriothesley succeeded to his father's earldom in 1581 and became a royal ward under the care of Lord Burghley. Educated at the University of Cambridge and at Gray's Inn, London, he was 17 years old when he was presented at court, where he was favoured by Queen Elizabeth I and befriended by Robert Devereux, 2nd earl of Essex. Southampton became a munificent patron of writers, including Barnabe Barnes, Thomas Nashe, and Gervase Markham, though he is best known as the patron of Shakespeare, who dedicated both *Venus and Adonis* and *The Rape of Lucrece* to him. It has been argued, albeit inconclusively, that Shakespeare's sonnets were addressed to him. If so, the earlier sonnets, urging marriage, must have been written before the beginning (in 1595) of Southampton's intrigue with Elizabeth Vernon, one of the queen's waiting women, which culminated with their hasty marriage in 1598, incurring the queen's wrath and leading to their brief imprisonment.

In 1596 and 1597 Southampton accompanied Essex on his expeditions to Cádiz and to the Azores. In 1599 he went to Ireland with Essex, but the queen insisted that Southampton return to London. He was deeply involved in the Essex rebellion (February 1601), on the eve of which he induced players at the Globe Theatre to revive *Richard II* (a play dealing with the deposition of a king) in order to stir up the populace. He was tried for treason on Feb. 19, 1601. His titles were forfeited and he was condemned to death, but his sentence was commuted to life imprisonment through the intervention of Sir Robert Cecil.

Portrait of Shakespearean patron, and possible object of affection, Henry Wriothesley, the earl of Southampton. Hulton Archive/Getty Images

On the accession of James I, Southampton resumed his place at court. He was made a Knight of the Garter and captain of the Isle of Wight in 1603 and was restored to the peerage by act of Parliament. In 1603 he entertained Queen Anne with a performance of Shakespeare's *Love's Labour's Lost* by the Lord Chamberlain's Men, soon to be known as the King's Men.

Southampton was an active member of the Virginia and East India companies. He was a volunteer in support of German Protestants in 1614, and in 1617 he proposed fitting out an expedition against the Barbary pirates. He became a privy councillor in 1619 but fell into disgrace through his determined opposition to the royal favourite, the duke of Buckingham. In 1624 he and his elder son volunteered to fight for the United Provinces against Spain, but on landing in the Netherlands they were attacked with fever, and Southampton died a few days after the death of his son.

SHAKESPEARE'S NONDRAMATIC POETRY

Shakespeare himself seems to have wanted to be a poet as much as he sought to succeed in the theatre. His plays are wonderfully and poetically written, often in blank verse. And when he experienced a pause in his theatrical career about 1592–94, the plague having closed down much theatrical activity, he wrote poems. *Venus and Adonis* and *The Rape of Lucrece* are the only works that Shakespeare seems to have shepherded through the printing process. Both owe a good deal to Ovid, the Classical poet whose writings Shakespeare encountered repeatedly in school. These two poems are the only works for which he wrote dedicatory prefaces. Both are to Henry Wriothesley, earl of Southampton. This young man, a favourite at court, seems to have encouraged Shakespeare and to have served for a brief time at least as his sponsor. An unreliable tradition supposes that Southampton gave Shakespeare the stake he needed to buy into the newly formed Lord Chamberlain's acting company in 1594.

Shakespeare may also have written at least some of his sonnets to Southampton, beginning in these same years of 1593–94 and continuing on through the decade and later. The question of autobiographical basis in the sonnets is much debated, but Southampton at least fits the portrait of a young gentleman who is being urged to marry and produce a family. (Southampton's family was eager that he do just this.) Whether the account of a strong, loving relationship between the poet and his gentleman friend is autobiographical is more difficult still to determine. As a narrative, the sonnet sequence tells of strong attachment, of jealousy, of grief at separation, of joy at being together and sharing beautiful experiences. The emphasis on the importance of poetry as a way of eternizing human achievement and of creating a lasting memory for the poet himself is appropriate to a friendship between a poet of modest social station and a friend who is better-born. When the sonnet sequence introduces the so-called dark lady, the narrative becomes one of painful and destructive jealousy. Scholars do not know the order in which the sonnets were composed—Shakespeare seems to have had no part in publishing them—but no order other than the order of publication has been proposed, and, as the sonnets stand, they tell a coherent and disturbing tale. The poet experiences sex as something that fills him with revulsion and remorse, at least in the lustful circumstances in which he encounters it. His attachment to the young man is a love relationship that sustains him at times more than the love of the dark lady can do, and yet this loving friendship also dooms the poet to disappointment and self-hatred. Whether the sequence reflects any circumstances in Shakespeare's personal life, it certainly is told with an immediacy and dramatic power that bespeak an extraordinary gift for seeing into the human heart and its sorrows.

SHAKESPEARE AND THE SONNET

A fixed verse form of Italian origin having 14 lines that rhyme according to a prescribed scheme, the sonnet is unique among poetic forms in Western literature in that it retained its appeal for five centuries and beyond. The form seems to have originated in the 13th century among the Sicilian school of court poets, who were influenced by the love poetry of Provençal troubadours. From there it spread to Tuscany, where it reached its highest expression in the 14th century in the poems of Petrarch. His *Canzoniere*—a sequence of poems including 317 sonnets,

Portrait of the Tuscan poet Petrarch, a master of the sonnet. The Petrarchan sonnet is named for him. Another form, the English sonnet, is also called the Shakespearean sonnet. Imagno/Hulton Archive/Getty Images

addressed to his idealized beloved, Laura—established and perfected the Petrarchan (or Italian) sonnet, which remains one of the two principal sonnet forms, as well as the one most widely used. The other major form is the Shakespearean (or English) sonnet.

The Petrarchan sonnet characteristically treats its theme in two parts. The first eight lines, the octave, state a problem, ask a question, or express an emotional tension. The last six lines, the sestet, resolve the problem, answer the question, or relieve the tension. The octave is rhymed *abbaabba.* The rhyme scheme of the sestet varies; it may be *cdecde, cdccdc,* or *cdedce.* The Petrarchan sonnet became a major influence on European poetry. It soon became naturalized in Spain, Portugal, and France and was introduced to Poland, whence it spread to other Slavic literatures. In most cases the form was adapted to the staple metre of the language—e.g., the alexandrine (12-syllable iambic line) in France and iambic pentameter in English.

The sonnet was introduced to England, along with other Italian verse forms, by Sir Thomas Wyatt and Henry Howard, earl of Surrey, in the 16th century. The new forms precipitated the great Elizabethan flowering of lyric poetry, and the period marks the peak of the sonnet's English popularity. In the course of adapting the Italian form to a language less rich in rhymes, the Elizabethans gradually arrived at the distinctive English sonnet, which is composed of three quatrains, each having an independent rhyme scheme, and is ended with a rhymed couplet.

The rhyme scheme of the English sonnet is *abab cdcd efef gg.* Its greater number of rhymes makes it a less demanding form than the Petrarchan sonnet, but this is offset by the difficulty presented by the couplet, which must summarize the impact of the preceding quatrains with the compressed force of a Greek epigram. An example is Shakespeare's Sonnet 116:

ELIZABETHAN LYRIC

Virtually every Elizabethan poet tried his hand at the lyric. Few, if any, failed to write one that is not still anthologized today. The fashion for interspersing prose fiction with lyric interludes, begun in the *Arcadia*, was continued by Robert Greene and Thomas Lodge (notably in the latter's *Rosalynde*, the source for Shakespeare's *As You Like It*, and in the theatres plays of every kind were diversified by songs both popular and courtly. Fine examples are in the plays of Jonson, John Lyly, George Peele, Thomas Nashe, and Thomas Dekker (though all, of course, are outshone by Shakespeare's).

The most important influence on lyric poetry, though, was the outstanding richness of late Tudor and Jacobean music, in both the native tradition of expressive lute song, represented by John Dowland and Robert Johnson, and the complex Italianate madrigal newly imported by William Byrd and Thomas Morley. The foremost talent among lyricists, Thomas Campion, was a composer as well as a poet; his songs (four *Books of Airs*, 1601–17) are unsurpassed for their clarity, harmoniousness, and rhythmic subtlety. Even the work of a lesser talent, however, such as Nicholas Breton, is remarkable for the suggestion of depth and poise in the slightest performances; the smoothness and apparent spontaneity of the Elizabethan lyric conceal a consciously ordered and laboured artifice, attentive to decorum and rhetorical fitness. These are not personal but public pieces, intended for singing and governed by a sense of beauty and art in which delight is a means of addressing the moral sense, harmonizing and attuning the auditor's mind to the discipline of reason and virtue. This necessitates a deliberate narrowing of scope—to the readily comprehensible situations of pastoral or Petrarchan hope and despair—and makes for a certain uniformity of effect, albeit an agreeable one. The lesser talents are well displayed in the miscellanies *The Phoenix Nest* (1593), *England's Helicon* (1600), and *A Poetical Rhapsody* (1602).

Let me not to the marriage of true minds
Admit impediments. Love is not love
Which alters when it alteration finds,
Or bends with the remover to remove:
Oh, no! it is an ever-fixéd mark,
That looks on tempests and is never shaken;
It is the star to every wandering bark,
Whose worth's unknown, although his height
be taken.
Love's not Time's fool, though rosy lips and
cheeks
Within his bending sickle's compass come;
Love alters not with his brief hours and weeks,
But bears it out even to the edge of doom.
If this be error and upon me proved,
I never writ, nor no man ever loved.

The typical Elizabethan use of the sonnet was in a sequence of love poems in the manner of Petrarch. Although each sonnet was an independent poem, partly conventional in content and partly self-revelatory, the sequence had the added interest of providing something of a narrative development. Among the notable Elizabethan sequences are Sir Philip Sidney's *Astrophel and Stella*, Samuel Daniel's *Delia*, Michael Drayton's *Idea's Mirrour*, and Edmund Spenser's *Amoretti*. The last-named work uses a common variant of the sonnet (known as Spenserian) that follows the English quatrain and couplet pattern but resembles the Italian in using a linked rhyme scheme: *abab bcbc cdcd ee.* Shakespeare's sonnet sequence—addressed to a "fair youth" and a woman known to critics as the "dark lady"—is perhaps the greatest of all. These sonnets purport to tell a love story, but the poet's underlying reflections on time and art, growth and decay, and fame and fortune are in many ways more memorable.

In its subsequent development the sonnet was to depart even further from themes of love. By the time John Donne wrote his religious sonnets (*c.* 1610) and Milton wrote sonnets on political and religious subjects or on personal themes such as his blindness (i.e., "When I consider how my light is spent"), the sonnet had been extended to embrace nearly all the subjects of poetry.

THE OBJECT OF THE POET'S AFFECTIONS

The sonnets have long provoked questions regarding Shakespeare's sexual nature. Like so many circumstances of Shakespeare's personal life, this question is shrouded in uncertainty. At age 18, in 1582, he married Anne Hathaway, a woman who was eight years older than he. Their first child, Susanna, was born on May 26, 1583, about six months after the marriage ceremony. A license had been issued for the marriage on Nov. 27, 1582, with only one reading (instead of the usual three) of the banns, or announcement of the intent to marry in order to give any party the opportunity to raise any potential legal objections. This procedure and the swift arrival of the couple's first child suggest that the pregnancy was unplanned, as it was certainly premarital. The marriage thus appears to have been a "shotgun" wedding. Anne gave birth some 21 months after the arrival of Susanna to twins, named Hamnet and Judith, who were christened on Feb. 2, 1585. Thereafter William and Anne

An illustration from Hutchinson's Story of the British Nation *depicting William Shakespeare courting Anne Hathaway.* Private Collection/ The Stapleton Collection/The Bridgeman Art Library

had no more children. They remained married until his death in 1616.

Scholars have wondered whether the couple were compatible, or if Shakespeare lived apart from Anne for most of their married life by design. The facts are tantalizingly inconclusive. When he moved to London at some point between 1585 and 1592, he did not take his family with him. He bought a fine house for his family in Stratford and acquired real estate in the vicinity. He had lived apart from his wife and children, except presumably for occasional visits in the course of a very busy professional life, for at least two decades. He seems to have retired to Stratford from London about 1612. He was eventually buried in Holy Trinity Church in Stratford, where Anne joined him in 1623. His bequeathing in his last will and testament of his "second best bed" to Anne, with no further mention of her name in that document, has suggested to many scholars that the marriage was a disappointment necessitated by an unplanned pregnancy. Divorce was nearly impossible in this era.

What was Shakespeare's love life like during those decades in London, apart from his family? Knowledge on this subject is uncertain at best. According to an entry dated March 13, 1602, in the commonplace book of a law student named John Manningham, Shakespeare had a brief affair after he happened to overhear a female citizen at a performance of *Richard III* making an assignation with Richard Burbage, the leading actor of the acting company to which Shakespeare also belonged. Taking advantage of having overheard their conversation, Shakespeare allegedly hastened to the place where the assignation had been arranged, was "entertained" by the woman, and was "at his game" when Burbage showed up. When a message was brought that "Richard the Third" had arrived,

Shakespeare is supposed to have "caused return to be made that William the Conqueror was before Richard the Third. Shakespeare's name William."

This diary entry of Manningham's must be regarded with much skepticism, since it is verified by no other evidence and since it may simply speak to the timeless truth that actors are regarded as free spirits and bohemians. Indeed, the story was so amusing that it was retold, embellished, and printed in Thomas Likes's *A General View of the Stage* (1759) well before Manningham's diary was discovered. It does at least suggest, at any rate, that Manningham imagined it to be true that Shakespeare was heterosexual and not averse to an occasional infidelity to his marriage vows. The film *Shakespeare in Love* (1998) plays amusedly with this idea in its purely fictional presentation of Shakespeare's torchy affair with a young woman named Viola De Lesseps, who was eager to become a player in a professional acting company and who inspired Shakespeare in his writing of *Romeo and Juliet* — indeed, giving him some of his best lines.

Apart from these intriguing circumstances, little evidence survives other than the poems and plays that Shakespeare wrote. Can anything be learned from them? The sonnets, written perhaps over an extended period from the early 1590s into the 1600s, chronicle a deeply loving relationship between the speaker of the sonnets and a well-born young man. At times the poet-speaker is greatly sustained and comforted by a love that seems reciprocal. More often, the relationship is one that is troubled by painful absences, by jealousies, by the poet's perception that other writers are winning the young man's affection, and finally by the deep unhappiness of an outright desertion in which the young man takes away from the poet-speaker the dark-haired beauty whose sexual favours the poet-speaker has enjoyed (though not without some revulsion at his own unbridled lust, as in Sonnet 129).

This narrative would seem to posit heterosexual desire in the poet-speaker, even if of a troubled and guilty sort, but do the earlier sonnets suggest also a desire for the young man? The relationship is portrayed as indeed deeply emotional and dependent; the poet-speaker cannot live without his friend and that friend's returning the love that the poet-speaker so ardently feels. Yet readers today cannot easily tell whether that love is aimed at physical completion. Indeed, Sonnet 20 seems to deny that possibility by insisting that Nature's having equipped the friend with "one thing to my purpose nothing"—that is, a penis—means that physical sex must be regarded as solely in the province of the friend's relationship with women: "But since she [Nature] pricked thee out for women's pleasure, / Mine be thy love and thy love's use their treasure." The bawdy pun on "pricked" underscores the sexual meaning of the sonnet's concluding couplet. Critic Joseph Pequigney has argued at length

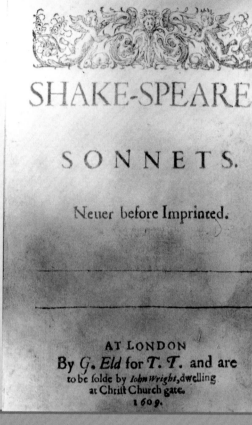

The cover of the first edition of Shakespeare's sonnets. The compilation is believed to have been published without Shakespeare's involvement. Hulton Archive/Getty Images

that the sonnets nonetheless do commemorate a consummated physical relationship between the poet-speaker and the friend, but most commentators have backed away from such a bold assertion.

A significant difficulty is that one cannot be sure that the sonnets are autobiographical. Shakespeare is such a masterful dramatist that one can easily imagine him creating such an intriguing story line as the basis for his sonnet sequence. Then, too, are the sonnets printed in the order that Shakespeare would have intended? He seems not to have been involved in their publication in 1609, long after most of them had been written. Even so, one can perhaps ask why such a story would have appealed to Shakespeare, and begs the question as to whether or not there is a level at which fantasy and dreamwork may be involved.

Chapter 5

MUSIC IN SHAKESPEARE'S PLAYS

Shakespeare's approach to music is perhaps less evident in his history plays than in his other dramatic types. Nevertheless, his love for and understanding of music and his mastery of the lyric is an appropriate consideration for the subject at hand.

It was customary in Tudor and Stuart drama to include at least one song in every play. Only the most profound tragedies, in accordance with Senecan models, occasionally eschewed all music except for the sounds of trumpets and drums. In his later tragedies, William Shakespeare defied this orthodoxy and used songs startlingly and movingly, particularly in *Othello*, *King Lear*, and *Hamlet*.

Dramas produced at court were invariably much more lavish than those put on by the professional companies. Casts were larger, as were the instrumental ensembles used to accompany songs and provide incidental music. *Gorboduc* (1561) by Thomas Sackville and Thomas Norton, the first English five-act drama in blank verse, used a five-part instrumental ensemble to accompany the dumb shows that introduced each act. *Wit and Science* (c. 1539) by John Redford provided as an interlude a composition played and sung by four allegorical characters. The sententious choirboy dramas presented at court throughout the second half of the 16th century were acted and sung by two companies, the Children of Paul's and the

Gentlemen and Children of the Chapel Royal. Most of these plays included a lament to be sung by a treble voice and accompanied by a consort of viols. About eight of these pieces survive; several are sufficiently lovely to justify their dreary alliterative verse. Shakespeare parodies the genre mercilessly in the Pyramus and Thisbe interlude performed by the rustics in *A Midsummer Night's Dream*; the blissfully absurd lament "What dreadful dole is here?" is a send-up of "Gulchardo," a consort song that has survived into the 21st century.

THE VOCAL MUSIC

The professional companies that put on plays in the public theatres worked with much-reduced musical resources. Normally, one boy actor could sing and perhaps play an instrument. Adult actors, especially those specializing in clown roles, sang as well. A special musical-comic genre, the jigg, was the particular domain of the great Shakespearean comedians Richard Tarlton and William Kempe. Jiggs (bawdy, half-improvised low-comedy burlesques) were put on at the conclusion of a history play or tragedy. They involved from two to five characters, were sung to popular melodies (such as "Walsingham" and "Rowland"), and were accompanied by the fiddle or cittern (a small wire-strung instrument strummed with a pick). Touring troupes created a vogue for jiggs on the Continent beginning in the 1590s. As a result, we have marvelous settings of jigg tunes by Jan Pieterszoon Sweelinck, Samuel Scheidt, and other important northern European composers. The most accomplished of the comedians was Robert Armin, who joined the Chamberlain's Men about 1598.

To what sorts of characters did Shakespeare assign most of the singing? Servants (both children and adults), clowns, fools, rogues, and minor personalities. Major figures

Illustrated sheet music for a version of the song "O mistress mine," which appears in Shakespeare's Twelfth Night. *Experts have debated whether the song's lyrics are by Shakespeare or someone else.* Time & Life Pictures/Getty Images

never sing, except when in disguise or in distracted mental states. Most songs, in fact, are addressed to the protagonists themselves.

It is thought that the boys' songs in commercial plays were often set pieces, drawn from a repertoire of

music suitable to a variety of dramatic situations. Thus, in *Antony and Cleopatra* the boy musician of the company sings a generic drinking song, "Come, thou monarch of the vine" (for which there is no surviving melody). Another boy, who was sufficiently famous for his name to have been included in the stage directions of the First Folio of 1623—he was Jacke Wilson—sang "Sigh no more, ladies" in *Much Ado About Nothing*. There is some debate about whether "Take, O, take those lips away" from *Measure for Measure* and "O mistress mine" from *Twelfth Night* predate these plays. The lyrics seem to most experts to be authentically Shakespearean, but there is the hint of an unperformed second verse to "Take, O, take," and instrumental settings of "O mistress" by William Byrd and Thomas Morley do indeed antedate the first production of *Twelfth Night*. It is reasonable to conclude that Shakespeare both made use of songs that were established in the popular repertoire of the period and composed his own lyrics as well. In both cases, the songs in his plays never seem to be extraneous, though their reasons for being there can be complex.

Shakespeare used vocal music to evoke mood, as in "Come, thou monarch," and, while doing so, to provide ironic commentary on plot or character. "O mistress," sung by Robert Armin in the role of Feste, is directed toward the aging Sir Toby Belch and Sir Andrew Aguecheek; the lyrics touch on all the themes of the play and even hint at Viola's transgendered disguise in the phrase "that can sing both high and low." The incantatory, magical, and ritual uses of song are also central to such plays as *A Midsummer Night's Dream*, *The Tempest*, and *Macbeth*. In the first, the fairies use "You spotted snakes" as a sleep-inducing charm, while in *The Tempest*, Ariel's song "Come unto these yellow sands" reassures the shipwrecked arrivals in Prospero's magical realm. The heavily magical-musical Weird Sisters' (Three Witches') scenes in *Macbeth* were so popular that they were greatly expanded in Restoration revivals of the play. Songs of the ritual type usually occur near the conclusion of a play; at the end of *A Midsummer Night's Dream*, for example, Titania calls upon the fairies to "First, rehearse your song by rote, / To each word a warbling note. / Hand in hand, with fairy grace, / Will we sing, and bless this place." Juno's song "Honour, riches" in Act IV, scene 1, of *The Tempest* is clearly the ritual blessing of a marriage and a charm incanted to produce fruitfulness.

Shakespeare also used songs to establish the character or mental state of the singer. Ariel simply describes himself in "Where the bee sucks." Iago uses songs to give himself the appearance of a rough soldier. Most significantly, Ophelia's snatches of folk song demonstrate the regressive breakdown of her personality. (The only other Shakespeare heroine who sings is Desdemona. To overwhelming effect, she sings a popular tune, "The Willow Song"—for which 16th-century words and music exist—just before she is murdered by Othello.) In *King Lear* Edgar feigns madness by singing snatches of folk song.

Other types of vocal music that appeared in the plays include serenades, part-songs, rounds, and catches, all used very much in imitation of real life in Renaissance England.

INSTRUMENTAL MUSIC

The instrumental forces available to Shakespeare were, for the most part, fairly sparse. Exceptions were the plays produced at court. *Twelfth Night* was first performed at Whitehall on Twelfth Night, 1601, as part of a traditional royal celebration of the holiday. *The Tempest* was given two court performances, the first in 1611 at Whitehall and the second in 1613 for the wedding festivities of the Princess Elizabeth and the elector palatine. Both plays contain nearly three times the amount of music normally present in the plays. For these special occasions, Shakespeare probably had access to court singers and instrumentalists. A more typical Globe Theatre production would have made do with a trumpeter, another wind player who doubtless doubled on shawm (a double-reed ancestor of the oboe, called "hoboy" in the First Folio stage directions), flute, and recorders. Textual evidence points to the availability of two string players who were competent at the violin, viol, and lute. A few plays, notably *Romeo and Juliet*, *The Two Gentlemen of Verona*, and *Cymbeline*, indicate specific consorts (ensembles) of instruments. More commonly, a stage direction will simply state that music is played. Small onstage bands accompanied serenades, dances, and masques. Offstage, they provided interludes between acts and "atmosphere" music to establish the emotional climate of a scene, very much as film music does today. "Solemn," "strange," or "still" music accompanied pageants and the magical actions in *The Tempest*.

Certain instruments had symbolic significance for Elizabethans. Hoboys (oboes) were ill winds that blew no good; their sounds presaged doom or disaster. They heralded the evil banquets in *Titus Andronicus* and *Macbeth* and accompanied the vision of the eight kings in the great witches' scene of the latter play. Hoboys provided a grim overture to the dumb show in *Hamlet*.

The sounds of the lute and viol were perceived by Elizabethans to act as benign forces over the human spirit; like musical homeopathy, they eased melancholy by

A painting depicting a scene from Twelfth Night *that shows musicians performing onstage* (background and foreground, right). The Bridgeman Art Library/Getty Images

transforming it into exquisite art. In *Much Ado*, as a prelude to Jacke Wilson's singing of "Sigh no more, ladies," Benedick observes: "Is it not strange that cheeps' guts [the strings of an instrument] should hale souls out of men's bodies?" The viol was becoming a very popular gentleman's instrument at the turn of the 17th century, challenging the primacy of the lute. Henry Peacham, in *The Compleat Gentleman* (1622), urges the young and socially ambitious to be able to "sing your part sure, and at first sight, withall, to play the same upon your viol, or the exercise of the lute, privately, to your self." It was probably the trendiness of the viol that attracted Sir Andrew Aguecheek to the instrument.

Not a single note of instrumental music from the Shakespeare plays has been preserved, with the possible exception of the witches' dances from *Macbeth*, which are thought to have been borrowed from a contemporary masque. Even descriptions of the kinds of music to be played are sparse. Trumpets sounded "flourishes," "sennets," and "tuckets." A flourish was a short blast of notes. The words *sennet* and *tucket* were English manglings of the Italian terms *sonata* and *toccata*. These were longer pieces, though still probably improvised. "Doleful dumps" were melancholy pieces (of which a few are still preserved) usually composed over a repeated bass line. "Measures" were dance steps of various sorts. The commonest court dances of the period were the pavane, a stately walking dance; the almain, a brisker walking dance; the galliard, a vigorous leaping dance in triple time, of which Queen Elizabeth was particularly fond; and the branle, or brawl, an easy circle dance.

THE AUTHENTICITY OF THE SONGS

The problem of authenticity plagues most of the vocal music as well. Barely a dozen of the songs exist in contemporary settings, and not all of them are known to have been used in Shakespeare's own productions. For example, the famous Thomas Morley version of "It was a lover and his lass" is a very ungratefully arranged lute song. In *As You Like It* the song was sung, rather badly it seems, by two pages, probably children. Some of the most important

Portrait of composer John Wilson, a musical associate of Shakespeare's. Some experts speculate that Wilson may have been Jacke Wilson, a young singer whose name appears in First Folio stage directions. Hulton Archive/Getty Images

and beloved lyrics, such as "Sigh no more, ladies," "Who is Silvia?," and, saddest of all, "Come away, death," are no longer attached to their melodies. It is believed that, in addition to Morley, two other composers, Robert Johnson and John Wilson (probably the selfsame Jacke Wilson who sang "Sigh no more" in *Much Ado About Nothing* and "Take, O, take" in *Measure for Measure*), had some association with Shakespeare at the end of his career. As soon as public theatre moved indoors, this frustrating state of preservation

ROBERT JOHNSON

(b. *c.* 1583, England—d. *c.* 1633, London, England)

Robert Johnson was believed to be the son of John Johnson, a composer who was also a lutenist to Elizabeth I. From 1596 to 1603 Robert was indentured to Sir George Carey, 2nd Lord Hunsdon, and during this time he began studying music. He later became a court musician, serving as lutenist to James I and later Charles I, and in 1628 he was named to the post of composer for the "lute and voices." His successor was appointed on Nov. 26, 1633, leading modern scholars to speculate that Johnson died shortly before that date.

About 1607 Johnson began working with Shakespeare's company, the King's Men, an opportunity that likely came about through his relationship with Carey, who had earlier served as the theatrical company's patron. Johnson wrote a number of ayres (solo songs featuring lute accompaniment) for several of Shakespeare's plays, including *Cymbeline* and *The Winter's Tale*. "Full fathom five" and "Where the bee sucks," perhaps his best-known songs, are from *The Tempest*. He also provided music for John Webster's *The Duchess of Malfi* (*c.* 1612/13) and a number of plays by Francis Beaumont and John Fletcher. Typically declamatory in style, Johnson's ayres drew praise for their ability to establish character and mood. His compositions for the lute, of which about 20 are extant, were written for the 9- or 10-course Renaissance lute and utilized the instrument's full range. Johnson also collaborated, often with Ben Jonson, on music for court masques, and his other works include dances, catches, and anthems.

changed; there are examples of at least 50 intact songs from the plays of Francis Beaumont and John Fletcher and their contemporaries, many of them composed by Johnson and Wilson.

MUSICAL REFERENCE AS A DRAMATIC DEVICE

In addition to performed vocal music, Shakespeare used all kinds of music and musical instruments referentially. The folk song and ballad tunes he quoted so frequently were equally well known to the groundlings as to the more distinguished patrons. Scraps of these tunes were used to create in-jokes and to evoke other sentiments as well. The pathos of Ophelia's madness was increased with the knowledge, which probably went back to childhood, of the folk songs she croons in her distraction. A favourite device of the playwright was to turn the lyrics of a popular song into a bantering dialogue between characters. A classic instance of this technique is the scene between the clown Peter and the household musicians in *Romeo and Juliet* (Act IV, scene 5). Peter first begs them to play "Heart's ease" and "My heart is full of woe," both well-loved popular tunes. Then Peter challenges the musicians Simon Catling, Hugh Rebeck, and James Soundpost to an interpretive debate over a fusty old lyric from *The Garden of Dainty Devices* (1576).

> When griping griefs the heart doth wound,
> And doleful dumps the mind oppress,
> Then music with her silver sound—

Peter then banters with the players, asking them whether "silver sound" refers to the sweet sound of silver—that is, money. The old lyric concludes:

> Is wont with speed to give redress,
> Of troubled mind for every sore,
> Sweet music hath a salve therefore.

Shakespeare depended on the audience's prior knowledge of the verse to give meaning and pathos to this otherwise rather bizarre interchange.

Shakespeare used musical instruments and their playing techniques as the basis for sexual double entendre or extended metaphor. A fine example of the former can be found in Act II, scene 3, of *Cymbeline*, where Cloten reports: "I am advised to give her music o' mornings; they say it will penetrate." The musicians enter, and Cloten continues: "Come on, tune. If you can penetrate her with your fingering, so; we'll try with tongue too." The best-known instance of extended metaphor is Hamlet's warning to Rosencrantz and Guildenstern against trying to manipulate him, couched in the language of recorder technique (Act III, scene 2). He says:

> You would play upon me, you would seem to know my stops, you would pluck out the heart of my mystery, you would sound me from my lowest note to the top of my compass, and there is much music, excellent voice, in this little organ, yet cannot you make it speak.

SHAKESPEARE'S MUSICAL ETHOS

There is very little evidence to be found in the texts themselves to show that Shakespeare had any particular knowledge of the art music of the period. He makes no allusions to the magnificent church polyphony being written at the time by William Byrd and his contemporaries or to the brilliantly witty madrigals of Thomas Weelkes and John Wilbye. The complexity of such music was perhaps inappropriate to outdoor theatrical performance and above the heads of most of Shakespeare's audience. Extant Elizabethan and Jacobean theatre music is simple and vivid, almost Baroque in style. Shakespeare may even have had some antipathy for that most famous of melancholic musicians, John Dowland; his portrayal in *Twelfth Night* of Duke Orsino's rather superficial taste for the "dying fall" surely must refer to the opening strain of Dowland's "Flow My Tears."

On the other hand, the playwright seems to have had a genuine fondness for honest English popular and traditional songs. He would never have taken the extraordinary step of giving "The Willow Song" to Desdemona in her hour of crisis if he did not believe in its emotional validity. Shakespeare certainly had a profound comprehension of the Renaissance Neoplatonic idea of the "music of the spheres" and the effect of both heavenly and earthly harmonies on the health of the human spirit. Perhaps his loveliest evocation of this concept comes from Act V, scene 1, of *The Merchant of Venice*, where Lorenzo speaks:

> Here will we sit and let the sounds of music
> Creep in our ears. Soft stillness and the night
> Become the touches of sweet harmony.
> Sit, Jessica. Look how the floor of heaven
> Is thick inlaid with patens of bright gold.
> There's not the smallest orb which thou behold'st
> But in his motion like an angel sings,
> Still choiring to the young-eyed cherubins.
> Such harmony is in immortal souls,
> But whilst this muddy vesture of decay
> Doth grossly close it in, we cannot hear it.

Lorenzo goes on to describe the calming effect of Orpheus's music on wild beasts:

Since naught so stockish, hard, and full of rage
But music for the time doth change his nature.
The man that hath no music in himself,
Nor is not moved with concord of sweet sounds,
Is fit for treasons, stratagems, and spoils;
The motions of his spirit are dull as night
And his affections dark as Erebus.
Let no such man be trusted. Mark the music.

CONCLUSION

Shakespeare was in the forefront of the development of the history, or chronicle, play as a genre. With his immeasurable gifts, he took one example and crafted many memorable dramas. In Shakespeare's hands the history play became much more than a dramatization of history. He presented intelligent and complex characters who reflect on the meaning of governance and kingship. He examined a multiplicity of matters such as the causes and consequences of a monarch's weakness, the nature of malevolence and the human capacity for evil, and the ultimate results of tyranny and opportunism. Still, philosophical reflections were not all he offered. Shakespeare knew how to keep his audiences engaged. Interspersed in his histories are tender love scenes, bawdy humour, and inspiring patriotism as well. There is, as many critics have said, something for everyone in Shakespeare.

What is even more remarkable than Shakespeare's ability to discover the dramatic potential in his subjects is his ability to lay out his plots in a gorgeous poetic voice. Readers familiar with the King James Version of the Bible find there echoes of the language Shakespeare himself spoke—language of sometimes breathtaking cadence and tremendous power. This gift of language is also evident in Shakespeare's nondramatic poetry. It is there in *Venus and Adonis* and *The Rape of Lucrece*, and it is amply evident in the sonnets.

Taken together with his tragedies and comedies and the other plays not so easily classified, Shakespeare's histories and poems (including the lyrics set to music) provide a richly creative vein of material that has been mined in many languages for more than four centuries. Indeed it would be difficult to imagine English literature—and theatre—in the absence of Shakespeare and his works.

anarchy A state of lawlessness or political disorder.

astute Marked by keen insight and clever awareness.

banish To send away from one's home or country by order of the ruling authority.

bawdy Humorously improper or lewd.

courtesan A prostitute whose clients were wealthy noblemen or members of the court.

crony A longstanding, close friend.

debauchery Extreme indulgence in sensual pursuits, such as drinking, eating, or sexual activity.

effeminacy Exhibiting qualities and characteristics usually connected to women; being overly delicate or refined.

ethos The distinguishing character, sentiment, moral nature, or guiding beliefs of a person, group, or institution.

factionalism A state characterized by contentiousness within a party or group.

folio A book printed on large sheets of paper folded in such a way to make two leaves of a book or manuscript.

foment To promote the growth or development of an idea or action.

germane Something that is relevant and appropriate or fitting.

malevolent Having, showing, or arising from intense often vicious ill-will or hatred.

narrative poem A poem that tells a story or relates an event.

octavo A book published on a piece of paper cut eight from a sheet.

opportunism Taking advantage of opportunities or circumstances, often with little regard for principles or consequences.

partisan One who acts on a firm belief in a party, faction, cause, or person.

profligate Wildly extravagant; spending one's time or wealth in a carefree and irresponsible manner.

quarto A book published on a piece of paper cut four from a sheet.

satyr One who is given to abnormal or excessive cravings for sex.

sonnet A fixed verse form of poetry consisting of 14 lines that rhyme according to a prescribed scheme.

sundry Various and assorted.

tetralogy A group of four dramatic pieces presented consecutively.

wastrel One who expends, or foolishly wastes, his or her resources.

$\mathcal{A}$mong modern editions of Shakespeare's works are Stanley Wells and Gary Taylor (eds.), *William Shakespeare, The Complete Works*, 2nd ed. (2005); G. Blakemore Evans and J.J. Tobin (eds.), *The Riverside Shakespeare*, 2nd ed. (1997); David Bevington (ed.), *The Complete Works of Shakespeare*, 6th ed. (2009); and Stephen Greenblatt (ed.), *The Norton Shakespeare*, 2nd ed. (2008). Three major scholarly series were in progress at the turn of the 21st century, with plays and poems in individual volumes: Stanley Wells (ed.), *The Oxford Shakespeare* (1982–); Philip Brockbank (ed.), *The New Cambridge Shakespeare* (1984–); and Richard Proudfoot, Ann Thompson, H.R. Woudhuysen, and David Scott Kastan (eds.), *The Arden Shakespeare*, 3rd series (1995–).

A number of works focus on the history plays in particular. These include Michael Hattaway (ed.), *The Cambridge Companion to Shakespeare's History Plays* (2002); Warren I. Chernaik, *The Cambridge Introduction to Shakespeare's History Plays* (2007); Phyllis Rackin, *Stages of History: Shakespeare's English Chronicles* (1990); John Julius Norwich, *Shakespeare's Kings: The Great Plays and the History of England in the Middle Ages, 1337–1485* (1999); Peter Saccio, *Shakespeare's English Kings: History, Chronicle, and Drama*, 2nd ed. (2000); Graham Holderness, *Shakespeare: The Histories* (2000); and Harold Bloom (ed.), *William Shakespeare: Histories*, new ed. (2009).

Dominique Goy-Blanquet, *Shakespeare's Early History Plays: From Chronicle to Stage* (2003), focuses on the first tetralogy. Among the works that approach the plays from a special perspective are Jean E. Howard and Phyllis Rackin,

Engendering a Nation: A Feminist Account of Shakespeare's English Histories (1997), part of a Feminist Readings of Shakespeare series; A.J. Hoenselaars (ed.), *Shakespeare's History Plays: Performance, Translation, and Adaptation in Britain and Abroad* (2004); Nicholas Grene, *Shakespeare's Serial History Plays* (2002); Wolfgang Iser, *Staging Politics: The Lasting Impact of Shakespeare's Histories* (1993), translated from German by David Henry Wilson; W.F. Bolton, *Shakespeare's English: Language in the History Plays* (1992); Paola Pugliatti, *Shakespeare the Historian* (1996); Stephen Orgel and Sean Keilen (eds.), *Shakespeare and History* (1999); Dick Riley, *Shakespeare's Consuls, Cardinals, and Kings: The Real History Behind the Plays* (2008); and Keith Dockray, *William Shakespeare, the Wars of the Roses and the Historians* (2002).

Maurice Charney, *All of Shakespeare* (1993), discusses each of the plays as well as the long poems and the sonnets. A valuable work on the sonnet form that includes a discussion of selected Shakespeare sonnets is Stephen Burt and David Mikics, *The Art of the Sonnet* (2010). The Arden series includes Katherine Duncan-Jones and H.R. Woudhuysen (eds.), *Shakespeare's Poems: Venus and Adonis, The Rape of Lucrece, and the Shorter Poems* (2007). Also useful are Michael Schoenfeldt, *The Cambridge Introduction to Shakespeare's Poetry* (2010); Patrick Cheney (ed.), *The Cambridge Companion to Shakespeare's Poetry* (2007); Dennis Kay, *William Shakespeare: Sonnets and Poems* (1998); Harold Bloom (ed.), *Shakespeare's Sonnets and Poems* (1999); Colin Burrow (ed.), *The Complete Sonnets and Poems* (2002); Peter Hyland, *An Introduction to Shakespeare's Poems* (2003); and A.D. Cousins, *Shakespeare's Sonnets and Narrative Poems* (2000). One of the most extensive treatments of Shakespeare's sonnets is Helen Vendler, *The Art of Shakespeare's Sonnets* (1997), which includes a compact disc of Vendler reading the sonnets. Other works that narrow the focus to Shakespeare's sonnets alone are Paul Edmondson and Stanley Wells, *Shakespeare's Sonnets* (2004); and David West, *Shakespeare's Sonnets* (2007). All the poems except the sonnets are treated in John Roe (ed.), *The Poems*, updated ed. (2006).

Index